Martin Cohen is an academic and author specializing in popular books in philosophy, social science, and politics, including *101 Philosophy Problems* and *Critical Thinking Skills for Dummies*. Other recent books include a look at how scientists work called *Paradigm Shift* and *I Think Therefore I Eat*. He has both researched and taught at universities in the UK, France, and Australia.

To Milo

Martin Cohen

THE AH-HA MOMENT

Exploring Philosophical Ideas through Jokes and Puzzles

AUSTIN MACAULEY PUBLISHERS

LONDON ∗ CAMBRIDGE ∗ NEW YORK ∗ SHARJAH

Ordering Information
Quantity sales: Special discounts are available on quantity purchases by corporations, associations, and others. For details, contact the publisher at the address below.

Publisher's Cataloging-in-Publication data
Cohen, Martin
The Ah-Ha Moment

ISBN 9781685628987 (Paperback)
ISBN 9781685628994 (ePub e-book)

Library of Congress Control Number: 2024912152

www.austinmacauley.com/us

First Published 2024
Austin Macauley Publishers LLC
40 Wall Street, 33rd Floor, Suite 3302
New York, NY 10005
USA

mail-usa@austinmacauley.com
+1 (646) 5125767

I should like to thank the team at Austin Macauley Publishers for all their help, enthusiasm, and professionalism.

And a very special thanks to Zolumio for the wonderful philosophical portraits on the cover. They capture just the spirit of the book – and maybe an unappreciated side of the philosophers too.

Table of Contents

Introduction

Here's a riddle to start the book off:

What kind of book is full of jokes—and yet is not a joke book?

Give up? Well, the answer is…a book about jokes. My riddle has the same structure as many more humorous ones, but isn't in fact funny. But don't worry; I've found plenty of jokes that are. In fact, I have had to do that in order to try to investigate essentially philosophical questions like:

- Why do we find certain things make us laugh?
- What purpose do jokes have in human society?
- And how can we make use of jokes and humor in our own lives?

After all, make no mistake, wit, humor, jest—call it what you will—is a crucial part of life today, both as individuals and collectively. We admire wit, and a "sense of humor" is cited as a valuable asset in both job adverts and dating profiles. Indeed, NOT having a sense of fun is something no one wants to admit. Of all the professors I've known over the years, invariably the ones who were the wittiest were also the ones who were the most original and creative thinkers. That said, there are different kinds of wit, just as there are different kinds of writing and conversation. Working out what makes something funny is like trying to nail a jelly…?

In Neil Simon's play, *The Sunshine Boys*[1], Simon expounds on his own theory of laughter:

---

[1] **Introduction:** Neil 1973, 15

"Words with a "k" in them are funny. Alkaseltzer is funny. Chicken is funny. Pickle is funny. All with a "k". 'L's are not funny. 'M's are not funny. Cupcakes are funny. Tomatoes are not funny. Lettuce is not funny. Cucumber is funny. Cab is funny. Cockroaches are funny—not if you get 'em, only if you say 'em."

Clearly, it's not quite as simple as that. Yet the investigation is worth undertaking because laughter is the cement that draws us together and makes moments that might otherwise be unremarkable sparkle.

In 2003, Rod Martin, a psychologist formerly of the University of Western Ontario, devised something called the Humor Styles Questionnaire (Psycho-tests.com), considered nowadays to be the first scientifically validated measure of your sense of humor. The questionnaire, like all good Sunday magazine quizzes, confidently places you in one of four categories:

- Affiliative,
- Self-Enhancing,
- Aggressive,
- and …
- Self-Defeating.

Ooh, er! You don't want to end up in the wrong category. Scary or not, today, it's in common use all over the world, although not *yet* on dating sites.

Less alarmingly, in 2008, Daniel Howrigan of the University of Colorado at Boulder claimed to have shown that intelligence and wittiness were two sides of the same coin. He asked nearly 200 people to create humorous statements and draw funny images. Those who scored higher on a test of general intelligence were also rated by observers as being significantly funnier[2].

Add to which, when the US recruitment company, Robert Half, conducted a survey in 2017, they found that 84% of respondents felt that people with a good sense of humor did a better job, while 91% of executives believed that a sense of humor was important for career advancement[3].

---

[2] Howrigan and MacDonald 2008
[3] RobertHalf 2017

And it's a cliché, but let's not forget that having a GSOH is supposed to be the first thing women look for in a man. Don't jump on me for putting that in a "sexist" way, because (a) humor doesn't respect political correctness and (b) there really is what researchers call a "humor gap". This is despite men and women being equally funny.

It shouldn't really surprise anyone, but men and women seem to be equally good at coming up with jokes. When, in 2009, Kim Edwards, a Ph.D. student in psychology at the University of Western Ontario, asked men and women to come up with funny captions for single-frame cartoons, both genders created an equal number of highly rated captions[4].

Writing in *The Scientific American* (October 1, 2012), Christie Nicholson recalls what happened after researchers at Western University, Canada, asked 127 men and women to select pairs of potential partners for either a one-night stand, a date, a short-term relationship, a long-term relationship, or friendship. In each pair, one partner was described as receptive to the participant's humor but not very funny themselves, and the other partner was described as hilarious but not all that interested in the participant's own witty remarks.

If the aim was to find friendship, women liked men who were witty even if they were not particularly receptive to their own jokes, but in every context, men wanted women who would laugh at their jokes rather than those who cracked their own ones. It was a very clear research finding: women looked for partners who amused them rather than ones who would appreciate their wit.

So, it seems that men and women use humor and laughter to attract one another and signal romantic interest, but each gender accomplishes this in a different way. At the outset, men use jokes as deer use antlers—as a courtship display. Later on, however, and as the relationship progresses, the role of humor changes: in a successful relationship, it becomes more about bonding, shared jokes, and also a means of smoothing over rough patches. "In fact, humor is rarely about anything funny at all; rather, sharing a laugh can bring people closer together and even predict compatibility over the long haul," writes Nicholson. In a stressed relationship, though, humor can add fuel to the flames. One or other partner (actually, Nicholson claims the problem is more or less confined to "men", but I think all of us know, just from school, that females can use humor negatively too) may use jokes to mock and disparage—

---

[4] PsychCentral 2011

or even just to avoid genuine communication. When the joke works, though, it's a complementary relationship, and one that researchers believe has deep evolutionary roots and likely serves a core reproductive purpose.

Indeed, as long ago as 1872, Charles Darwin described chimpanzees giggling as they played.

"If a young chimpanzee is tickled—and the armpits are particularly sensitive to tickling, as in the case of our children—a more decided chuckling or laughing sound is uttered, though the laughter is sometimes noiseless. The corners of the mouth are then drawn backward, and this sometimes causes the lower eyelids to be slightly wrinkled. But this wrinkling, which is so characteristic of our own laughter, is more plainly seen in some other monkeys. The teeth in the upper jaw of the chimpanzee are not exposed when they utter their laughing noise, in which respect they differ from us. But their eyes sparkle and grow brighter." [5]

That's from a little-known essay called 'On the Expression of Emotions in Man and Animals.' Darwin goes on to note there:

"The imagination is sometimes said to be tickled by a ludicrous idea, and this so-called tickling of the mind is curiously analogous with that of the body. Everyone knows how immoderately children laugh and how their whole bodies are convulsed when they are tickled. The anthropoid apes, as we have seen, likewise utter a reiterated sound, corresponding with our laughter, when they are tickled, especially under the armpits."

Darwin links laughter and humor appreciation to the development of higher-order thinking. Given all that, maybe it's time that being funny is taught in school—as a kind of life skill! If it were, I think we'd all find that the ability to tell a joke is actually a lot more demanding than the ability to rote-learn facts or methods. Well, it is if you invent the joke anyway. Naturally, most jokes are borrowed from who knows where, with their origins a bit of a mystery. But I actually kind of like that fact.

But in the absence of compulsory jokes education, here's a slim book that tweaks the curtain on the hidden, shared world of wit, jest, and humor—call it what you will. One reason is, well, just for fun. But a weightier reason is that jokes are a way into profound truths about how we think, how we live with each other, and even about philosophy. Philosophy? Well, yes, jokes play with

_____

[5] Darwin 1872, 133

language, truth, and logic and can do so rather better than the philosophers usually manage.

You see, we spend all our lives being told that jokes and humor are not serious, and that only serious things matter. But in many ways, intelligence, wit, and creativity are all linked.

That's why *The Scientific American* firmly stated in a feature in 2012, 'It's time to take a serious look at humor,' and why they valiantly made a stab at it[6]. Although predictably being "scientists" they seemed to struggle with some of the subtleties of what makes us laugh. In fact, there's only a couple of really insightful studies of jokes over the centuries, and they're all by philosophers— if we reunite psychology as a branch of philosophy for a moment.

There's Sigmund Freud's slim book *Wit and Its Relation to the Unconscious[7],* which starts:

"Some may inquire whether the subject of wit is worthy of such effort. In my opinion, there is no doubt about it."

It's over a hundred years old now, but the book is a timeless analysis of how and why we find things humorous. Investigating the phenomenon fitted in with Freud's interests in the hidden workings of our minds in general, and sure enough, he ends up saying that humor satisfies an unconscious desire to escape everyday stresses and to release us, at least momentarily, from our inhibitions. Call it the Stand-Up Comedy Club rationale. (I look at the particular humor of stand-up in Chapter 6.)

Less well-known is a book by the French philosopher Henri Bergson. His account, simply called "Laughter," made him a cult figure in the late 19th and early 20th century, although he is much less well remembered now. Bergson was actually a contemporary of Freud's, and I think, probably inspired Freud's study, although Freud was fastidious in covering his theoretical debts. Certainly, *Laughter* came to many of the same conclusions about jokes, saying that humor was something distinctively human and also, at times, aggressive: "an unavowed intention to humiliate." But not so unavowed if you've ever been part of the audience at a comedy club!

Both Freud and Bergson treat humor as something to be studied, like infidelity or maybe depression. They are addressing humor as doctors treat a

---

[6] Nicholson 2012

[7] Freud 1922

social phenomenon. But there's another way to look at it, which is to see jokes as a rather wonderful kind of thinking skill that we all could do with a bit of.

After all, most of us rather admire people who can come up with quick one-liner, who can conjure up laughs effortlessly. Talking to *Time* Magazine about the New York comic Chris Rock some years ago, MTV president Judy McGrath surely echoed a common feeling when she suggested that such people "say everything you want to say but that you're not quite sharp or smart enough to think of yourself"[8]. McGrath's solution was to sign Rock up as a host. And Rock's secret? He says he talks about "subjects that aren't funny in the first place." There's an insight there if we can but make use of it.

Rock hit the headlines in 2022 when a cheeky (off-color) joke he made at the Oscars provoked Will Smith to leave his seat, climb on the stage, and hit Rock in the face! He then returned to his seat in front of a shocked audience and shouted menacing threats. Comedian and director Judd Apatow tweeted excitedly that the display represented "pure out of control rage and violence", which it did, but the episode also underlined something else: that jokes are tied up with power relations. Which is why when Rock carried on with his slot despite the assault, he showed not only professionalism but a different kind of strength.

Actually, Rock also offers practical tips for how to actually create jokes, not just tell them. He went on in that *Time* Magazine interview (Farley 1999) to explain that his comic ideas begin as "cumulus clouds of general observation" before turning into the thunder and lightning of his stand-up routine. The example he offers is this: "I had something the other day—this thing about men—that no matter what they're doing at their job, if some beautiful woman walks by, you try to do it cool. So, I'm trying to figure out how you make unloading a garbage truck cool—or whatever. Notes like that are what I leave for myself."

Okay, it's not very funny, put like that, but nonetheless, it's a practical piece of advice that underlines that there are simple tricks we can all use to bolster our lurking comic skills. Starting with reading this book!

Similarly, a careful compilation of jokes (along with an unmatched ability to tell them) is what made Ronald Reagan one of America's most effective presidents, and his style is worth a detailed look at later in this book. Just

---

[8] Farley 1999

recently, when the Russians launched their invasion of Ukraine, they publicly mocked its president, in part because they knew him from Russian television already—as a joker. "Putin, I think, dismissed Zelensky as a clown and an idiot," Misha Bondarenko told *The Hill* magazine[9]. Bondarenko, who was born and raised in Ukraine, adds of the Russian leader: "I think his psychological portrait of Zelensky was someone who would give up at the first sign of trouble." If so, now the world knows better. After all, comics include, in their number, many tough-minded as well as smart people. He has his critics, but Volodymyr Zelensky displayed the qualities of empathy, strategy, and intuition that combine to make a great leader, whereas Vladimir Putin, a man even his most loyal supporters could not say has much of a sense of fun, has displayed exactly the opposite.

Because, when you meet wit, you know it is closely linked to intelligence. Not, maybe, the kind of intelligence that gets you through exams, but certainly the kind that provides an extra boost throughout life. And that is, surely, more important.

---

[9] Seals 2022

Chapter 1
Serious Jokes

A stern-looking Sigmund Freud graces the cover of TIME Magazine in 1924.

Ludwig Wittgenstein, the splendidly dour 20th century philosopher, usually admired for trying to make language more logical, once remarked, in his earnest Eastern European way, that a *serious work* in philosophy could consist entirely of jokes[10]. This caused a great *furor*, or 'an outbreak of public anger or excitement,' at the time, with much raising of eyebrows and even some polite coughing, and his fellow philosophers have wondered ever since, in paradoxical fashion, whether the remark was in itself a joke. But in fact, the clue is in the emphasis on being "serious". For Wittgenstein spotted earlier than anyone else that there is a particular quality to jokes, which makes them the ideal vehicle to explore the big issues of how language works, how logic misleads, and even clues as to what we might do about it.

---

[10] Malcolm 2001, 28

In fact, humor often involves a sudden, unexpected shift in perspective, forcing a rapid reassessment of assumptions. Philosophy, at its best, does much the same thing. That said, the great philosophers have been slow, perplexed, and generally ineffectual in their efforts to examine even something that they have clearly recognized as a crucial social phenomenon, and only a few seem to have seen humor's potential as a kind of intellectual can-opener.

The 19th century English essayist William Hazlitt seems to have been a rare thinker who really made a serious stab at just what it is about wit that is especially human by writing that:

'Man is the only animal that laughs and weeps, for he is the only animal that is struck with the difference between what things are and what they ought to be.' [11]

Dog owners might disagree, though. Indeed, not long after Hazlitt wrote this, Darwin was noting that "the gait and appearance of a dog when cheerful, and the marked antithesis presented by the same animal when dejected and disappointed, with his head, ears, body, tail, and chops drooping, and eyes dull. Under the expectation of any great pleasure, dogs bound and jump about in an extravagant manner and bark, for joy."

On the Expression of Emotions in Man and Animals[12].

You're unlikely to have ever come across these writings, though. Better known is what Sigmund Freud wrote, in his short and remarkable book, *Wit and Its Relation to the Unconscious*:

'Whoever has had occasion to examine that part of the literature of aesthetics and psychology dealing with the nature and affinities of wit will, no doubt, concede that our philosophical inquiries have not been awarded to wit for the important role that it plays in our mental life.'[13]

Freud seems to feel that certain elements of humor can be identified, but they seem more like symptoms of a syndrome—let us not say a 'disease'! than an actual diagnosis. Jokes are 'only disjointed fragments, which we should like to see welded into an organic whole.'

---

[11] Hazlitt 1819, 2

[12] Darwin 1899, 115

[13] Freud 1922, 3

Alas, Freud notes drily: 'it is rather remarkable how few examples of recognized witticisms suffice the authors for their investigations and how each one accepts the ones used by his predecessors.'

And so, to avoid that error straightaway, here's a joke to start the book off:

Joke #1: Baldy

Three men—a totally bald cook nicknamed "Baldy", a very learned professor called "Brains", and a barber with a thick black beard—were going on a long journey and had to camp out at night. They decided to take it in shifts to watch over their valuables. The barber took the first one, but soon got bored. So to pass the time, he shaved the head of the professor—and then woke him up to take his turn on the second shift. The professor got up, rubbed his head in puzzlement, and then exclaimed, 'What an idiot you are, barber' he said, 'you've woken up Baldy instead of me!'

It's not such a great joke, agreed, but incredibly, given its contemporary feel, it's one of the oldest jokes around. This is, we might say, a joke with a pedigree. A version of it appears in the *Philogelos*, or *Laughter Lover*, which is a collection of some 265 jokes written in Greek and compiled some 1,600 odd years ago[14]. And yet, indisputably, despite its antiquity, the style of this and at least some of the other jokes is very familiar, even if they are peopled with different stereotypes.

Rather than "Irishmen" or "mothers-in-laws", the favorite targets of the authors of the *Laughter Lover* are people from Abdera (a city that is today on the border of Bulgaria and Greece and presumably not far back then from where the book was being written) and men with bad breath. Alongside are the *scholasticos*, or absent-minded professors, along with the eunuchs. Not immediately tempted by any of these themes? But try another timeless example about 'the dinner party joke' that pops up in the *Laughter Lover*[15], in various forms.

---

[14] Hierocles 1983, 11

[15] *Hierocles* 1983, 14

Joke #2: The Joke Book

A traveler is staying at a monastery, where the Order has a vow of silence and can only speak at the evening meal. On his first night, while they are eating, one of the monks stands up and shouts, 'Twenty-two!' Immediately, the rest of the monks break out into raucous laughter. Then they return to a new silence. A little while later, another shouts out 'One hundred and ten' to even more uproarious mirth. This goes on for two more nights with no real conversation, just different numbers being shouted out, followed by ribald laughing and much downing of ale. At last, no longer able to contain his curiosity, the traveler asks the Abbot what it is all about.

The Abbot explains that the monastery has only one non-religious book in it, which consists of a series of jokes each headed with its own number. Since all the monks know them by heart, instead of telling the jokes, they just call out the number.

Hearing this, the traveler decides to take a look at the book for himself. He goes to the library and carefully makes a note of the numbers of several of the funniest jokes. Then, that evening, he stands up and calls out the number of his favorite joke—which is "seventy-six". But nobody laughs; instead, there is an embarrassed silence.

The next night he tries again. 'One hundred and thirteen!' he exclaims loudly into silence, but still no response. After the meal, he asks the Abbott if the jokes he picked were not considered funny by the monks.

'Ooh no,' said the Abbott. 'The jokes are funny; it's just that some people don't know how to tell them!'

Okay, it's indeed an oldie, but I like it! And the joke seems to draw on something common to all people and demonstrate that humor is something that transcends communities and periods in history. Yet jokes are also clearly things rooted in their time and place. Recall too that, at the time of this joke, monks and secret books were serious business. Perhaps the most important philosophical observation to make and principle to note is that both of these jokes involve one of those 'ah-ha!' moments.

Yet is the investigation of humor worth serious people's time and effort? Of that, Friedrich Nietzsche[16], at least, had no doubt, writing:

---

[16] Nietzsche 1998, 175

"I would actually go so far as to rank philosophers according to the level of their laughter—right up to those who are capable of golden laughter. And assuming that gods, too, are able to philosophize, as various of my conclusions force me to believe, then I do not doubt that when they do so, they know how to laugh in a new and superhuman fashion—and at the expense of everything serious! Gods like to jeer; it seems that even at religious observances, they cannot keep from laughing."

– Friedrich Nietzsche, *Beyond Good and Evil*

Freud comes to the same conclusion, but by a very different route, insisting that 'there is an intimate connection between all psychic occurrences, a connection which promises to furnish a psychological insight into a sphere which, although remote, will nevertheless be of considerable value to the other spheres.'

So, consider another revealing anecdote told about Wittgenstein. (There are lots, and even some quite juicy ones involving piles of gold and Nazis!) The story starts with the great philosopher conversing with another brainy bod, the Italian economist, Piero Sraffa, in his Cambridge rooms about the logical and grammatical structures necessary for communication. (This is the least of what goes on in private university rooms when no one is around.) Anyway, it seems that as Wittgenstein concluded his description of the workings of language, Sraffa stroked his chin with his fingers and asked, 'Well, now, my friend, what is the logical structure of this?' The implicit challenge: well, what is the "grammar" of a gesture? We all know that they can convey very clear messages. Wittgenstein, who for decades had insisted on the need for logical structures, experienced a shock to his philosophical system (an "ah-ha" moment!) such that it is said to have resulted in him abandoning all his work to that date and instead adopting an entirely new approach.

Just fancy that. But the story also provides a good example, as Freud says, of why we should take jokes very seriously. Which is why this book is also about why we should do that, as well as take them a bit more philosophically— to weed out the good ones from the Marx brothers' ones.

The thing about jokes is that they often deny any serious purpose. A serious joke is a sort of contradiction in terms. Yet what makes a good joke funny is that it forces us to perceive incongruities: between the decorous and the low, between the ideal and the actual, between the logical and the absurd. The incongruity that amuses is that between an abstract concept and the real thing it represents. Don't accept lesser witticisms! Another great philosopher, Arthur Schopenhauer, says that it is our spotting of discrepancies between an abstract concept and the real thing that is the real reason for laughter.

Schopenhauer on Laughter

Arthur Schopenhauer's pioneering analysis of 'what makes us laugh' is both one of the most perceptive philosophical investigations and one of the most neglected. Because, for Schopenhauer, as for Wittgenstein two hundred years later, jokes are serious stuff—all about language and concepts. But let Schopenhauer explain it himself:

"This very incongruity of sensuous and abstract knowledge, on account of which the latter always merely approximates to the former, as mosaic approximates to painting, is the cause of a very remarkable phenomenon which, like reason itself, is peculiar to human nature, and of which the explanations that have ever anew been attempted, are insufficient. I mean laughter…the cause of laughter in every case is simply the sudden perception of the incongruity between a concept and the real objects that have been thought through in some way, and laughter itself is just the expression of this incongruity. It often occurs in this way: two or more real objects are thought through one concept, and the identity of the concept is transferred to the objects; it then becomes strikingly apparent from the entire difference of the objects in other respects that the concept was only applicable to them from a one-sided point of view. The greater and more glaring their incongruity with it, from another point of view, the greater the ludicrous effect that is produced by this contrast. All laughter is then occasioned by a paradox and therefore, by unexpected subsumption, whether this is expressed in words or in actions. This, briefly stated, is the true explanation of the ludicrous."

–*The World as Will and Idea*[17]

It is precisely this kind of thing that philosophers are supposed to be the experts at sniffing out. Indeed, I've structured the book loosely around some

---

[17] Schopenhauer, 76-7

of the staidest philosophical categories—logic, language, and ethics—but don't be misled by that. The key debates are much more general, about how we perceive and make sense of the world and other people, and the key insights are much more likely to be sociological or psychological. A bad reason to use philosophical terms is that I'm cocking a snook at the pretensions of twentieth century philosophy, with its pseudo-technicality and jargon, and there's surely no harm in that. But a better reason for emphasizing the philosophical aspects is that it helps to strip down the jokes to see both how they work and what that tells us about ourselves—both as individuals and as communities. In other words, the aim here is to use the tools of philosophy to investigate one of the defining features of humanity: our ability to enjoy, share, and tell jokes.

So, enough preambles, let's get sniffing! There are some great stories here, all of which have intriguing philosophical insight attached.

Most writers of jokes, wit, and humor agree that the common ingredient is a moment of insight. 'Things momentarily, if not ultimately, make sense,' writes Kenneth Lincoln, adding that when the artist Magritte wrote (below a painting of a pipe) *'Ceci, n'est pas un pipe,'* he was creating a classic humorist's conflict of ideas.

The contemporary American authors, Thomas Cathcart and Daniel Klein, have explored this and other issues in books like *Plato and a Platypus Walk into a Bar: Understanding Philosophy Through Jokes*[18]. This last book is not only entertaining but also a pioneering look behind the philosophy of humor. In the *Platypus*, they offer that:

'The construction and payoff of jokes and the construction and payoff of philosophical concepts are made out of the same stuff. They tease the mind in the same way. ...philosophy and jokes proceed from the same impulse: to confound our sense of the way things are, to flip our worlds upside down, and to ferret out hidden, often uncomfortable, truths about life. What the philosopher calls an insight, the gagster calls a *zinger*.'

Elsewhere, expanding on this idea in a newspaper interview, Klein said, 'We figured out that jokes and philosophy have a lot in common. Every joke has that "ah-ha"! moment.' And his co-author, Cathcart adds, 'One reason you laugh at a joke is that you are so delighted with yourself that after that split second, you 'got it.' There is that experience with philosophy—some ideas are

---

[18] Cathcart and Klein 2008, introduction

a little offbeat. You have that moment when you don't get it, and then you say, 'Oh, right!'"[19]

For the listener, what we accept one moment as making sense, we later perceive as perfect nonsense. Or vice versa. 'Thereby arises, in this case, the operation of the comic element,' explains Freud, speaking of humor in general and using the words of Theodor Lipps[20].

Freud also comments on the slightly different "ah-ha" moment—the moment when you crack a joke. This "Joke Moment" shows itself as an involuntary "inspiration" or a sudden flash of thought, Freud says. 'A moment before one cannot tell what kind of joke one is going to make, though it lacks only the words to clothe it. One usually experiences something indefinable, which I should like most to compare to an absence, or sudden drop of intellectual tension; then all of a sudden, the witticism appears, usually simultaneously with its verbal investment.'[21]

Alas, mainstream philosophy doesn't offer so many insights, so many 'ah-ha!' moments. It seems to have lost its way somewhere around the second century BCE. I say that because Plato's little playlets, the famous "dialogues", are littered with, if not exactly jokes, certainly witticisms, yet his follower, Aristotle, eschewed the form. Instead, Aristotle seems to have stressed the idea that it is also there in some of Plato's writings that such ambiguous, "deceptive" language is to be avoided and that the most powerful form of reasoning must be logical.

That said, Aristotle himself did write a whole book on comedy, but it is thought to have been lost. (It would have been the second book of the Poetics) And although, in *The Name of the Rose,* Umberto Eco describes a monk committing a string of murders to prevent a sole surviving copy of Aristotle's treatise, which he comes across in the abbey's labyrinthine library, from ever coming to light, the actual remnants of Aristotle's views are far from dramatic. In Umberto Eco's tale, the rediscovered book is dangerous because laughter, if properly understood, can be used to undermine the very foundations of religion and society, but within recent philosophy, the theory of laughter is thin gruel.

---

[19] Boston Globe 2007
[20] Freud 1922, 3
[21] Freud 1922, 265

If one or two of the classics of skeptical philosophy, such as the books of David Hume and Schopenhauer, are full of dry witticisms, mainstream philosophy is self-consciously dry and serious. Even so, there are lurking examples of wit in the most unexpected places, for instance in the 20th century philosopher Bertrand Russell's philosophy of mathematics. Here, in a book called *On Denoting*, Russell writes:

'By the law of the excluded middle, either "A is B" or "A is not B" must be true. Hence, either "the present King of France is bald" or 'the present King of France is not bald' must be true. Yet if we enumerated the things that are bald and then the things that are not bald, we should not find the present King of France in either list. Hegelians, who love synthesis, will probably conclude that he wears a wig.'

To understand why this counts as funny, you have to have plowed through the rest of the book. This "poverty of philosophy", if I might borrow a phrase from Marx himself (who had no use for jokes either), is reflected in works like *The Blackwell Companion to Philosophy*, a lengthy and self-consciously encyclopedic work, which gives the topic of laughter and humor just one paragraph, calling it a psychological phenomenon, 'which has a variety of objects, moods, and institutional settings'[22]. Well, maybe it does, but don't pitch for a regular slot on TV with that as your starting line!

The academic, Robert Sharpe, observes, evidently without being able to do anything about it, since the observations are in a correspondingly tiny entry for the *Oxford Companion to Philosophy*, that although laughter is like language, clearly one of the distinguishing features of humanity, philosophers have spent only a small proportion of their time and learned papers on it, particularly when contrasted with the volumes devoted to the philosophy of language. The philosopher whose theory of natural rights is said to be the basis of modern political theory, Thomas Hobbes, dismissed laughter as a nasty thing:

"…nothing else but sudden glory arising from sudden conception of some eminency in ourselves, by comparison with the infirmity of others, or with our own formerly."

– *On Human Nature*[23]

---

[22] Bunnin and Tsui-James 2008
[23] Hobbes 1650, Ch. 9, sect. 13

But perhaps the ancient Greek philosopher, Epicurus, who gives his name to an adjective, Epicurean, meaning something rather enjoyable, had already prejudged the matter for mainstream philosophy when he wrote in his *Lives of the Philosophers* as one of his 'letters' against anything that created mental confusion.

'So when we say that pleasure is the goal, we do not mean the pleasure of the dissipated and those that consist in having a good time, as some out of ignorance and disagreement of refusal to understand suppose that we do, but rather freedom from pain and disturbance in the soul.' (Letter to Menoeceus)

Ah yes, that's surely what most people mean by 'pleasure'! But cheerfully extending the breach between philosophers and everyone else, Epicurus, whose name rather confusingly we use to signify not so much 'good taste' as sensuous and luxurious living, then continues to his correspondent:

'For what produces the pleasant life is not continuous drinking and parties or pederasty (sexual activity involving a man and a boy) or womanizing or the enjoyment of fish and other dishes of an expensive table, but sober reasoning… which banishes the opinions that beset souls with great confusion…'

How did the writings of an advocate for 'sober reasoning' become a synonym for wild partying? And the answer is…, as this joke about Sherlock Holmes and Doctor Watson's camping trip so nicely illustrates, that as with most things in life, it's all about context. Logic can help you answer questions, but it can't help you ask the right ones. That requires something, perhaps both subtler and rarer: commonsense.

Joke #3: Sherlock Holmes Goes Camping…

The famous detective, Sherlock Holmes, and his indefatigable assistant, Mr. Watson, go on a camping trip. In the middle of the night, Holmes, ever a light sleeper, wakes up and stares up at the night sky with thousands of stars twinkling down on them.

Holmes, renowned for his own powers of deduction, leans over and nudges Watson, 'Watson! Wake up! Look around and tell me what you see!'

Watson rubs his eyes and says, 'Well, Holmes, I can see many countless millions of stars stretching away as far as the eye can see.'

'And what do you deduce from that?'

'Why…that the universe is incomprehensibly old and vast.'

'Very good, Watson! Is there anything else, though?'

'Uh, well, Holmes, yes, meteorologically speaking, I deduce that tomorrow will be slightly warmer than today with fine clear skies.'

'Excellent, Watson! But is there anything else—perhaps more practical—that we can deduce immediately?'

'Certainly Holmes. We can deduce from the position of the Great Bear that it is now a little after 3.00 a.m. Now what, may I ask, do you deduce, Holmes, and then please, can we go back to sleep?'

'Watson, you fool, the wind has blown our tent away!'

The philosophical takeaway here is invaluable: understanding the world hinges on having first adopted the right kind of perspective. It's a lesson that is also central to the success of many jokes.

The joke is doubly philosophical because all Watson's observations are logically "valid", but only Holmes's deduction is useful. The assumption is that we all know the difference, yet, if we do, it is by common sense, that most underrated of qualities. The lesson is that the important distinction is not between 'valid' and 'invalid' arguments (which is a mathematical matter any fool or computer can be taught to recognize) but between 'sound' and 'unsound' ones—a distinction that requires sensitivity to background knowledge and context. Yet how often do you hear people classifying positions as logical and illogical, as compared to sound and unsound? Logical language has the grandeur that we need jokes to provide an antidote to, to strip away the pretensions of those who offer sophisticated explanations for phenomena when simple ones will do. Philosophers beware!

So now let's take a closer look at jokes that subtly shed light on how we argue and reason. Because the great problem with real arguments, meaning the everyday arguments of politics or indeed between husband and wife in the home, is not that the positions adopted are "invalid", logically speaking, as per Aristotle and almost all the philosophy textbooks written afterwards, but rather that they start from the wrong point, using the wrong premises. *Jokes deliberately do this too.*

In real life, we ask the wrong question, like, 'Is it Bob's turn to do the washing-up?' and argue because "No", he did it yesterday, but maybe "Yes" too, because his partner just prepared and cooked the meal. Or, if you prefer something more formal, can logic prove that Socrates is mortal? "Yes", because Socrates is a man, and all men are mortal. So, is Sherlock Holmes mortal too, then? Uh, no. But he is certainly a man—just look in the book.

Which brings me to definitions and another joke, this time a very simple one, which is supposed to throw light on such things. It's a topic that Socrates regularly raised in the many conversations and dialogues recorded by Plato. But where Socrates would ask passersby questions like 'What is Justice' and 'What is Beauty?' here we start by trying to define things that seem, on the face of it, a lot more straightforward: some different kinds of animals.

Joke #4: What Is an Elephant?

What is an elephant?

An elephant is, like a horse, a four-legged animal that you can also ride on, but much bigger.

What is a fish?

A fish is an animal with no legs, unlike a horse, although there are some that have heads that look like horses called 'seahorses.'

What is a dog?

A dog is like a horse that has four legs, but it is smaller and hairier and barks.

Okay, okay, but now tell me what a horse is like.

A horse is a cross between an elephant, a fish, and a dog.

Well, you can't argue with that conclusion. As long as you accept the first three definitions (and they're not exactly 'wrong'), how can anyone fail to accept the fourth one too?

Personally, I quite like the joke, as I think it looks just pleasingly silly, but the 'What is an Elephant?' joke is also supposed to shed light on the Hegelian notion of universality. That's not the stuff of most comedy routines, so a quick *segue* may be helpful to see what that is all about and how it relates to definitions. And this is that the doughty German philosopher, Georg Wilhelm Friedrich Hegel (1770–1831), usually remembered for his claim to have discovered the fundamental law governing the evolution of human society, used to claim that the world consists of two opposed forces that continually battle each other before combining into a new, "universal", something with the attributes of both. His favorite example was the apparent contradiction of "being" and "not being". This contradiction, Hegel says, is reconciled in the state of *becoming*. Schopenhauer, his contemporary and fellow countryman, sneered at such talk, deriding this particular example as a great joke fit only for the lunatic asylum! (Nonetheless, since evidently it is a kind of joke, it is doubly worth a mention here…) However, Hegel's dialectical reasoning, to give it its grand name, caught other imaginations for other reasons. Marx and Engels began to see history as a series of such contradictions, with their chosen example being that of the workers and the bosses, with the result of the contradiction, the synthesis, being socialism.

Here in this unassuming (actually rather unfunny) little joke about defining animals, there is a gentle play with concepts, and the punch line delivers a curious rebuke to the ways we conventionally imagine knowledge can be built up. It wouldn't surprise Hegel, as he actually says of humor in a book called, dauntingly, *The Science of Logic*, that it is through contradiction that wit allows the true relationships and nature of things to show, or indeed shine through.

For the listener, what we accept one moment as making perfectly good sense, we later perceive as perfect nonsense. 'Thereby arises, in this case, the operation of the comic element,' explains Freud, speaking of humor in general.

However, although it's true that there are plenty of contradictions going on in Freud's little joke, I'm not convinced that much light is really shed on anything. Except, maybe, the nature of explanations, or more specifically, the problem with explanations that take the available evidence and force it to fit into a theory. And, of course, there's another joke that offers a special insight into problems like that.

Joke #5: The Policeman and the Drunk…

A New York cop approached a man in the street. The Englishman had evidently had a few too many and was alternately holding onto a lamp post and crawling slowly around it, looking intently at the ground. So the police officer went up to him and asked, 'Hey, what's the matter, brother?'

'I say, old top,' said the Englishman, 'It's a most extraordinary thing, but I've lost a dollar bill, and I can't find the bally thing.'

The officer helped him look for it, but as it was clear that there was no sign of it, he soon asked, 'Are you sure you lost it here?'

'Why, no?' answered the Englishman, 'I lost it over there, on Sunset Boulevard.'

'Then why on earth are you looking for it here?' asked the cop exasperatedly.

'Well, surely you can see, old chap, the light's much better here under the lamps!'

There are many versions of this 'The policeman saw a drunk...' joke, but the first versions seem to have appeared in newspapers in the United States in the 1930s. In more recent years, the joke has been so often cited in dry and learned discussions of research methodology that it has acquired its own name and a certain status. The so-called 'streetlight effect' is said to illustrate the risks of allowing practical considerations to skew research findings.

Because, indeed, something like the drunken search in the joke really does often go on in the real world. Scientists (maybe sometimes for very good reasons) don't investigate phenomena directly but rather create experimental set-ups that are supposed to be similar in crucial respects. For example, the vast bulk of medical and therapeutic testing follows the same pattern: products are tested not on people, which is complicated, dangerous, and expensive, but on mice. This is despite the fact that there is no reliable or predictable correspondence between how a mouse reacts, say, to an antibiotic, and how a human will.

Just like the drunk opting for the wrong street, pharmaceutical companies will test drugs for, say, their bacteria or inflammatory response properties on mice in the face of the fact that unlike humans, mice tolerate millions of live bacteria in their blood before the induction of severe inflammation or shock and are thousands of times more resistant to most inflammatory stimuli than humans. The results are a joke!

There's a spooky sounding drug called TGN1412 that illustrates the unfunny side too. In 2006, the drug was given to six healthy volunteers, tempted by a serious £2000 fee, much higher than for most trials. They were given doses that were far smaller than those that had previously been 'successfully' tested on—not mice—but pitiful crab-eating macaque monkeys. Just a few minutes after the last volunteer had been injected with his dose, the participant who had received the first one started to complain of headaches and, soon afterwards, fever and cramps. Soon, all the volunteers who had received the drug became ill, throwing up and complaining of severe pain[24].

Nonetheless, over the last 50 years, multiple types of treatments for cancer, atherosclerosis, autoimmune diseases, and many others have been tested on animals, usually mice, and then proclaimed as successfully proven to be both safe and efficacious...

But Officer, mice are totally different from humans! Shouldn't we be looking elsewhere? 'Ah yes, but surely you can see it's much more practical to test drugs on them...'

Here's another famous riddle that maybe offers guidance on how to frame and investigate questions to avoid later making profound and entirely mistakes. I've called this version 'Perceptual Spectacles' with a nod at the rose-tinted things that the wearing of which, as the great Kant himself observed, must but make everything in the world seem pink.

Joke #6: Perceptual Spectacles

Six prisoners are chained up in a dark cellar. After a while, they become aware that there must be a creature in there with them, but as it is totally dark, they can only tell what it is like by touching it. As they are chained up, each of them can only touch the bit nearest them.

The first prisoner says that the creature is like a very solid pillar.

The second, says that it is like a rope.

The third is that it is like a tree branch.

The fourth is that it is like a large floppy fan.

Fifth, that it is like a roughly finished water tank.

The sixth that it is like a smooth pipe.

What is the creature?

What is it? The creature is an elephant. The first prisoner felt its leg, the second its tail, the third its trunk, the fourth its ear, the fifth its belly, and the sixth one of its tusks.

The point of the story is that it appears in many different forms, (usually as a parable called "the Blind Men and the Elephant". but I adapted it to be

---

[24] Attarwala 2010

more riddlesome), usually centered on India, is that there can be many different views of the world and that *they are all equally true* but limited. Recall Watson's replies to Holmes while camping? It's not enough to be right; you have to be relevant too.

The ancients saw the tale as much more than just a parlor joke. Writing in "The Poetics", long, long ago too, Aristotle declared that we learn something deeper from riddles since:

"The very nature indeed of a riddle is this: to describe a fact in an impossible combination of words, which cannot be done with the real names for things but can be with their metaphorical substitutes."

For Aristotle, a riddle provides an unexpected and contradictory image, alternately saying that "this is so" and "this is not so". This contradiction surprises, bewilders, and helps uncover a hidden relationship beyond the paradox. It is this paradoxical element in the riddle or joke that conveys learning.

Likewise, a Buddhist version of the tale, which has the six men fiercely arguing about who is right, finishes:

O how they cling and wrangle, some who claim
For preachers and monks, the honored name!
For quarreling, each to his view, they cling.
Such folk see only one side of a thing.

The story of the 'Blend Men and the Elephant' has been used in contexts well beyond the traditional religious one. In physics, it has been seen as an analogy for wave-particle duality, the phenomenon that challenges core beliefs in modern physics because light appears, under certain conditions, to be able to behave both as a wave, and as a stream of particles at the same time. Which is impossible. The words of the great 20th century physicist, Werner Heisenberg, sum it up very well:

'We have to remember that what we observe is not nature in itself, but nature exposed to our method of questioning.'[25]

Writing in the middle of the 19th century, the American philosopher C. S. Peirce paraphrased Aristotle's way of equating riddles with 'the bogus word

---

[25] Heisenberg 1958, 58

coinages in jests,' but then took things a little further. He calls the learning that takes place in jokes and riddles 'the action of experience' and says that this action emerges as 'a series of surprises'[26]. Experience, Peirce says in one of his most quotable quotes, is a great teacher because she acts upon our minds with a series of surprises, bewildering our categories of thought, and making us learn.

Charles Sanders Peirce and the Papier Mâché House

C. S. Peirce (who pronounced his name 'purse' and lived from 1839–1914) was a philosopher, chemist, and polymath, now remembered mainly as a pioneer of the field of semiotics and for the formulation of the pragmatic maxim. He expressed it like this:

'Consider what effects, that might conceivably have practical bearings, we conceive the object of our conception to have. Then, our conception of these effects is the whole of our conception of the object.'[27]

As an individual, he seems to have been far from amusing, suffering from his late teens onward from a nervous condition that his biographer, Joseph Brent, says left him at times almost stupefied, and then 'aloof, cold, depressed, extremely suspicious, impatient of the slightest crossing, and subject to violent outbursts of temper.'

Peirce inherited a substantial amount of money, which he spent on a huge estate that he was then unable to afford to run. Efforts to obtain academic employment were stymied by personal animosities and rivalries. It is with this bitter background that we should read his much-quoted description of life as a series of bad jokes:

"In all the works on pedagogy that I ever read—and they have been many, big, and heavy—I don't remember that anyone has advocated a system of teaching by practical jokes, mostly cruel. That, however, describes the method of our great teacher, experience."[28]

At other times, too, Peirce writes of the value of "Pure Play", as "a lively exercise of one's powers [that] has no rules, except this very law of liberty".

---

[26] Houser 1992, 227

[27] *Collected Papers of Charles Sanders Peirce* (1891) volume 5, paragraphs 388–410

[28] Lecture II : The Universal Categories, § 2 : Struggle, *Collected Papers* (1891) Volume 5, paragraph 51

His term for this special kind of play is "musement", and he says it is an essential part of philosophical inquiry.

One time, for example, Peirce amused himself in his description of Descartes as marking the period when philosophy put off childish things and began to be a conceited young man. In another moment of levity, which perhaps also has merit as an analogy, Peirce describes the theory of 'nominalism' then making the rounds in British philosophy as being:

"…as if a man, being seized of a conviction that paper was a good material to make things of, were to go to work to build a papier mâché house, with roofing paper, windows of paraffined paper, chimneys, bathtubs, locks, etc. of different forms of paper…" [29].

The point being that the 'house' would be following a splendidly logical 'system' but of no use at all in practice.

Peirce goes on to say that the phenomenon of surprise itself, so central to a good joke, is 'in itself highly instructive'…because of the emphasis it puts upon a mode of consciousness that can be detected in all perceptions, namely, a *double consciousness*. And, in the following passage, I think maybe Peirce puts his finger on something profound. Discovery, knowledge, and experience all start with this "pedagogy of surprise".

"Imagine that your mind was filled with an imaginary object that was expected. At the moment when it was expected, the vividness of the representation was exalted, and suddenly, when it should have come, something quite different came instead. I ask you whether at that instant of surprise there is a double consciousness, on the one hand of an ego, which is simply the expected idea suddenly broken off, and on the other hand of the non-ego, which is the strange intruder, in his abrupt entrance."[30]

The surprise is not in the abrupt and unexpected experience. It is rather in the relationship between the known and the unknown; between the familiar and the new; or between the "expected idea" and the "strange intruder".

I think that the truth of this insight is demonstrated very well by this chapter's closing joke, one that superficially is about email etiquette, but that underneath allows the entrance of a "strange intruder". It illustrates Freud's point that the omission of elements in a narrative is one way to be witty. There's certainly a shift in perspective here, even a kind of surprise.

---

[29] *Collected Papers* (1891) Volume 6, paragraph 7
[30] Houser 1992, 154

Joke #7: Breaking News

A man who lives in a flat in a hot town center, goes on holiday, leaving his neighbor to water his prize bonsai tree and look after his dog. A few days later, the neighbor sends him an email to say his beloved bonsai tree has died.

The news spoils the man's holiday, and he writes back rather crossly to say that at the very least his neighbor might have led up to it more gradually, for example by saying that the tree is looking a bit thirsty and thus hinting that he was getting worried about it. The neighbor realizes he has been rather crass and apologizes profusely.

A week later, he emails to say that the weather had turned very hot and today the dog seemed a bit thirsty…

Chapter 2
Jokes About People and
How We Live Together

The French philosopher, Henri Bergson, not only dressed like Charlie Chaplin, but he also set out a theory of "mechanical movements" that predates and perfectly describes the American comic's method.

The French philosopher Henri Bergson, writing in the 19th century, thought that in order to understand humor, we must see its social function. However, sometimes it is not immediately evident. Take this little witticism.

Joke #8: The Elephant

Q: Why did the elephant stand on the marshmallow?
A: He didn't want to sink into the hot chocolate.

It seems that 'elephant jokes' first appeared in the United States in 1962. They were first recorded in the summer of 1962 in Texas and gradually spread across the U.S.[31]. A year later, elephant jokes were so ubiquitous that they could be found in newspaper columns and in magazines like *TIME* and *Seventeen*, with circulations of millions of people.

Seven years later, the sociologists Roger Abrahams and Alan Dundes, in a (1969) paper called 'On elephantasy and elephanticide,' declared elephant jokes to be convenient disguises for racism and claimed that the jokes symbolized the nervousness of white people about the civil rights movement. While blatantly racist jokes became less acceptable, elephant jokes were a useful proxy. 'Elephant joke cycles' in the 1960s were a covert way in which whites expressed their anxieties about racial integration and miscegenation.

Here, or at least for some sociologists, the humor comes from the fact that it is actually racist, with the elephant representing the black man in white society. The sociologists note that in some anthologies of slang, a marshmallow is a "middle-aged Caucasian: soft and white". They are not worried by the fact that, evidently, hardly anyone else knows this.

It seems a stretch to read all that into a little harmless joke about one of our favorite animals and a sweetie. But there are famous supporters who support just this kind of approach. Sigmund Freud himself famously presented humor as the device used by the unconscious mind to evade the restrictions imposed on it by the conscious. Freud, the Austrian father of "psychoanalysis", trained as a doctor but wrote in a letter (April 2, 1896):

'When I was young, the only thing I longed for was philosophical knowledge, and now that I am going over from medicine to psychology, I am in the process of attaining it'[32].

His 'big idea' was that early childhood experiences are repressed by a controlling, censorious ego into the shadowy depths of the Unconscious along with many subconscious desires. He ambitiously called this idea a kind of Copernican Revolution (after Copernicus' replacement of the Earth with the Sun as the center of the universe)—one that displaced the conscious mind from the center of the thinking universe. Jokes, as the famous psychoanalyst correctly notes, are often about sex or death. Wit, he says: 'puts itself in the service of but two tendencies, which may themselves be united under one

---

[31] Cray and Herzog 1967, 27–36
[32] Draenos 1978

viewpoint: either hostile wit serving as aggression, satire, or defense, or it is obscene wit serving as a sexual exhibition.'

Freud: The Viennese Joker

Sigismunf Schlomo Freud (to give him his real name) was born in Freiberg, now part of the Czech Republic, on the 6th of May 1856. That makes him a Taurus, a sign associated with jokesters including several of today's best-known stand-ups—John Oliver, Jerry Seinfeld, and George Carlin.

But likely you do not think of Freud as a comedian because, academically he started out (at age 17) in medicine, studying at the University of Vienna, graduating in 1881, and then working at Vienna General Hospital. It was here that he worked alongside Joseph Breuer to treat hysteria, a condition that included a mix of physical symptoms, such as blindness and loss of sensation, and more psychological ones, such as hallucinations and suggestibility.

In 1885, Freud went to Paris as a student of the French neurologist, Jean-Martin Charcot, and when he returned a year later, he set up his own private practice focusing on neuropsychiatry and nervous and brain disorders, all of which he treated through psychoanalysis, a term he coined in a book called Studies in Hysteria (1895). In 1899, he published his influential work on The Interpretation of Dreams, and in 1902, he was appointed Professor of Neuropathology at the University of Vienna, a post he would hold until 1938, when he was obliged to flee Europe from the Nazis.

Many of Freud's ideas can be traced back to Schopenhauer, even if he rarely acknowledges the debt. His book, The Ego and the Id (1923), for example, which he presents as offering a new structural model of the mind, essentially develops Schopenhauer's earlier insight.

Freud's approach to humor is similarly about the different 'levels' of consciousness. For Freud, jokes, like dreams, satisfy our unconscious desires. In the book of most interest to us here, called Wit and Its Relation to the Unconscious (1905), he seeks to show that jokes provide pleasure by releasing us from our inhibitions and allowing us to express sexual, aggressive, playful, or cynical instincts that would otherwise remain hidden.

Perhaps the best thing about this book is that, in the course of elaborating his theory, Freud provides a rich collection of jokes and anecdotes, thereby giving not just jokes, but the art of being funny itself, the attention it surely deserves.

Which brings me to Donald Trump's 'Locker Room Talk' during the presidential campaign in 2016, chatter that caused a political outcry.

'She was married. And I moved on from her very heavily. In fact, I took her out furniture shopping. She wanted to get some furniture,' I said, 'I'll show you where they have some nice furniture.' I moved on her like a bitch, but I couldn't get there. And she was married. Then, all of a sudden, I see her, she's now got the big phony tits and everything. She's totally changed her look.

'I've gotta use some tic-tacs, just in case I start kissing her. You know I'm automatically attracted to beautiful—I just start kissing them. It's like a magnet. Just kiss. I don't even wait. And when you're a star, they let you do it. You can do anything. Grab them by the…You can do anything.'

– The New Republic[33]

In the audio of the now-infamous conversation between Donald Trump and Billy Bush, a journalist who by 2016 was known to the public as an anchor on NBC's highly respected *Today* show, Bush can be heard laughing, participating approvingly, and making validating comments such as, 'Sheesh, your girl's hot as shit' and 'Yes! Yes, Donald has scored!'

Later, as a result of the comments and behavior revealed in the recording, Noah Oppenheim, the NBC executive in charge of the *Today* show, sent a memo to his staff that stressed that he was "deeply troubled" by the revelations. 'Let me be clear: There is simply no excuse for Billy's language and behavior on that tape,' he wrote. NBC has decided to suspend Billy pending further review of this matter.'[34]

Still later, according to *USA Today*, Billy Bush himself said that he was 'embarrassed and ashamed' about his role in that conversation. 'I was younger, less mature, and acted foolishly in playing along. I'm very sorry.' But the Donald himself showed no such contrition beyond a formulaic apology that was not quite apologetic, suggesting that this was how all red-blooded men talked. And the public, by and large, seemed to agree with him. But then, in all this, Trump showed his instinctive grasp of human nature.

---

[33] *The New Republic,* 2017
[34] huffpost.com 2016

Freud says that the smutty joke was originally directed against the woman and is comparable to an attempt at seduction. If a man tells or listens to obscene jokes in male society, the original situation, which cannot be realized on account of social inhibitions, is thereby also represented. Whoever laughs at a smutty joke, as Billy did with the Donald, does the same as the spectator who laughs at sexual aggression.

Freud is emphatic that such jokes are like the denudation of a person of the opposite sex toward whom the joke is directed. Is it a peculiarly male kind of humor? Or do women too mock men (for being too sexually fixated or for being perhaps insufficiently so?) in exclusively female groups, like the so-called 'hen parties?' Women consulted in the process of writing this book insist not, but then…maybe they would say that. Nonetheless, the protagonist that Freud presents as part of his analysis of 'the utterance of obscene words' does sound more like a man than a woman. He writes that 'the person' attacked is forced to picture the parts of the body in question, or the sexual act, and it is shown that the aggressor himself pictures the same thing. '…the sphere of the sexual or obscene offers the richest opportunities for gaining comic pleasure besides the pleasurable sexual stimulation, as it exposes the person's dependence on his physical needs (degradation) or it can uncover behind the spiritual love the physical demands of the same (unmasking.).' [35]

But let's not be too shocked to recognize the very real 'comic' skills that Trump displayed. After all, this is standard fare on comedy circuits.

Freud understood that sexually exciting speech changes into obscene wit as its own end; and becomes distinctly hostile and cruel, utilizing the sadistic components of the sexual impulse' against the psychological and social hindrance. He writes:

'It makes possible the gratification of a craving (lewd or hostile) despite a hindrance that stands in the way; it eludes the hindrance…'[36]

Surely this is part of the real appeal of comedy clubs, which are lubricated with alcohol and typically conducted in semi-darkness. All of this is about allowing the removal of normal social restraints and escaping normal rules. The relationship between male and female is one of the most tightly controlled social norms, and it is a favorite theme of stand-up comedians.

---

[35] Freud 1922, 360
[36] Freud 1922 146

As Freud wrote, 'Among rural people or in the ordinary hostelry, one can observe that not till the waitress or the hostess approaches the guests does the obscene wit come out; in a higher order of society, just the opposite happens; here, the presence of a woman puts an end to smutty talk. The men reserve this kind of conversation, which originally presupposed the presence of bashful women, until they are alone, 'by themselves'[37]. Thus, gradually, the spectator, now turned listener, takes the place of the woman as the object of the smutty joke.'

Which brings us back to United States President Number 44. Donald Trump broke a lot of social conventions for political reasons but was usually careful to present them as "only joking". When it came out, the real problem with Donald Trump's 'locker room humor' was that it was so unsophisticated, and the writers in the serious media were sophisticated people who did not find it *funny*. Freud again: 'Not until we come to the refined and cultured does the formal determination of wit arise. The obscenity becomes witty and is tolerated only if it is witty.'

And yet, Freud argues that when intellectuals laugh over a delicately obscene witticism, 'We laugh at the identical thing that causes laughter in the ill-bred man when he hears a coarse, obscene joke; in both cases, the pleasure comes from the same source. The coarse, obscene joke, however, could not incite us to laugh because it would cause us shame or would seem to us disgusting; we can laugh only when wit comes to our aid.'[38]

Fortunately for stand-up comedians everywhere, Freud explains, in all obscene jokes we succumb to striking mistakes of judgment about the 'goodness' of the joke as long as it satisfies the formal conditions; a lead-in, a concealed element, a punchline...'the technique of these jokes is often very poor while their laughing effect is enormous.'

This, one must note, is certainly very true of many drunken comedy night specials in clubs. One-liners like, I wonder what the chairs think about all day: 'Oh, here comes another asshole.'

Jokes like this are the staple fodder of stand-up comedy, benefiting from the sense that sexual innuendo and foul language are liberating. Or as the great political writer George Orwell (1903–1950) has put it in an essay for the

---

[37] Freud 1922, 143–4
[38] Freud 1922, 148

literary magazine *Horizon: A Review of Literature and Art,* called *The Art of Donald McGill* (1945):

"Whatever is funny is subversive; every joke is ultimately a custard pie… and a dirty joke is…a sort of mental revolution."[39]

Speaking of custard pies invites me to *disinter*, that is:

1. To dig up or remove from a grave or tomb; exhume.
2. Bring it to public notice; disclose…

The British comic Tommy Cooper is a stand-up comedian of a kind that would have been pretty familiar to Orwell. Even if Cooper is from a different era to ours, he still offers insights into how comedy "works".

First of all, Cooper didn't make up his own jokes. Incredibly, he complied with a library of maybe half a million of them from various sources, including another British comedian, Max Miller, and a US comic called Robert Orben, and later, as he became more successful, by hiring script writers. Cooper bought a strictly limited edition, typed copy of the 'Fun Master Encyclopedia of Gags' of jokes from another US comic, an ex-vaudevillian called Billy Glason, whose wit also ended up in the acts of Billy Carson, Bob Hope, and Ed Sullivan.

You see, jokes and jokesters are too different animals, to some extent requiring different skills.

Despite not inventing the jokes, Cooper, however, used his own natural sense of wit and timing to deliver them in significantly different styles and forms. (To some extent, I have followed this split in that I too have limited skills at generating jokes, but do like to refine and polish them.)

Anyway, Cooper, like Freud and Peirce, like professional comics everywhere, would carefully examine each joke to identify what made it funny. Typically for him, it was the element of a pun or play on words; sometimes it was a "visual" element—something Schopenhauer too picks out as a fine form of incongruity—sometimes it was a "lateral" element, meaning a twist that requires the information originally apprehended to be reexamined in a new light.

---

[39] Orwell.ru

Cooper would select from his research the most promising material and retype it, as I say, in his own words and style, and give it a heading like "Family Planning!!" or "Love bites!" the former presumably being considered funnier given the number of exclamation marks.

In Cooper's time, a lot of jokes relied on stereotyping women as stupid, especially the wife. A typical joke like this runs, "I took my wife on a cruise, and she left the laundry out of the pothole. She thought it was a washing machine!" The audience, which would have been predominantly middle-aged couples, shared this notion that wives were sillier than their husbands—the kind of shared this taboo prejudice that was being made explicit that again Freud identified as one of the sources of humor.

Plato and Laughter

It's often said that Plato frowned on jokes and humor generally, blurring the line between truth and falsehood. Certainly, two of Plato's dialogues—the *Republic* and the *Laws*—recommend regulations on comedy and laughter. In a third dialogue, *Philebus* warns that malicious laughter corrupts the soul, while a fourth, the *Apology*, pits Socrates against the comic poet Aristophanes, who maliciously convicts Socrates in the court of public opinion. The message here is that jokes are not only dangerous for the soul but also corrupt and distort society itself.

But, as with most of Plato, the truth is never that simple. Plato's views on laughter and comedy are more complex and more interesting. After all, Plato himself is something of a comic poet.

None of his plays survive intact, but the titles of thirty of them are known, including:

Pieces of Furniture
The Resident Aliens
Ants
and *Zeus Being Wronged*

A fragment of another play, simply called *Phaon*, the hero of which is a ferryman with a magic potion that makes him irresistible to women, includes a scene in which a character sits down to study a poem about gastronomy and reads some of it aloud:

"In ashes first your onions roast, until they are brown as toast, then with sauce and gravy cover; eat them, and you'll be strong all over."

And a moment later:

"Never cut up a sardine or mackerel of silvery sheen, lest the gods scorn a sinner such as you and spoil your dinner; but dress them whole and serve them up, and so you shall most richly sup."[40]

We can only rue the great loss of comedic material. At least, the fragments are enough to underline that Plato did not "really" deplore humor, even if some of his dialogues include characters doing just that. And in any case, there are striking stylistic and thematic similarities between Plato's dialogues and ancient Greek comedies. Plato's dialogues are sketches of contemporary figures, many of whom are clearly being ridiculed. (Such as Thrasymachus and Glaucon.)

The *Philebus*, the dialogue that contains Plato's most detailed discussion of laughter, includes the argument that laughing at people in the right way can foster learning and further human inquiry. It is in this dialogue, too, that there is the argument that subsequent academics have dubbed "superiority theory", that we enjoy laughing at the misfortune or failures of others both out of malice and out of the pleasure we gain from our implied superiority.

According to the so-called "superiority theory", one of the key factors in something being funny is its ability to make someone feel "superior" to someone else. The clown slipping on the banana skin is offering us a sense of our own superiority as well as presenting an absurd spectacle. Superiority theory explains why the CEO gets an appreciative titter when they give even the faintest bit of humor at the annual meeting, or why classes everywhere enjoy lecturer's jokes so much. In the question of 'How to be funny,' Rule Number 1 is high status. Research confirms the sad truth that we laugh at jokes told by our social superiors and resent jokes told by those we feel are our social interiors.

I prefer jokes that "punch up" rather than down, though, like the following one, where the target is experts rather than any more maligned group.

---

[40] Yonge 1853

Joke #9: The Channel Tunnel

The British and the French were discussing the Channel Tunnel. The Chief Engineer said, 'The idea is that to dig it, we'll send a thousand men to one end and a thousand men to the other end, and they'll meet in the middle.' Someone said, 'But suppose that the tunnels don't quite meet?' Then the engineer said, 'Then we'll have two tunnels.'

A lot of Cooper's jokes are about things he dreamed about, which underlines how I should imagine how jokes have one foot in the everyday world and one foot in our subconscious.

"The other night I dreamed I was eating a huge white marshmallow, as big as a thousand ordinary ones! It was really chewy and took ages to eat. Anyway, the dream was so realistic that I woke up in a sweat. The trouble was, afterwards, I had trouble getting back to sleep as the pillow had gone."

But let's hear now from a more contemporary jokester. In an interview with the *New York Times* in 2013, celebrating her achievements as a stand-up comedian, the American humorist, Sarah Silverman, recalls how her routine included a joke about how she was licking jelly off her boyfriend (let's not go into details), and then the thought suddenly struck her: 'Oh my god, I'm becoming like my mother!'

Humor is there in the unexpected shift, yes, but the intimate reference to sex is what gives the joke its "effect". If she had told a story about how, one day, she was peeling potatoes in the kitchen for a meal and then suddenly thought, 'Oh my god, I'm becoming like my mother!' I don't suppose the crowd would have laughed so much. But you never know, stand-up comedy is an alcohol-fueled affair, and pretty much the 'form' of a joke often suffices, whatever the content. (The reader might like to try the two versions out.)

No, the joke here seems to rely on the socially created notion of "mothers" as sensible, conservative creatures who not only don't do, but never have done, naughty sex, and it is this classic clash of different assumptions that creates humor.

In any case, Ms. Silverman puts sex central to her whole approach to comedy, revealing to the *Times* reporter that what originally attracted her to the activity was that she had lost her virginity to a comedian. 'I was attracted to funny people,' she quips at the end of the interview.

Sex is taboo, but it is also important for another reason. It's something we are all intimately involved with. The nineteenth century French thinker Henri Bergson, one of the few philosophers of humor, wrote that laughter is always connected to humans or to something that can in turn be connected to humans. "A landscape", he points out, 'may be beautiful, inviting, magnificent, drab, or repulsive; but it is never funny.' By contrast, he says:

'You may laugh at a hat, but what you are making fun of, in this case, is not the piece of felt or straw, but the shape that men have given it: the human caprice whose mold it has assumed.'[41]

Well, that's not a great example, and disappointingly, it doesn't contain in it any humorous aspect, which may point at why Bergson is not considered today as exactly an A-list philosopher, but even so, he was in his time highly influential. His big idea, which he opposed to the new "mechanistic" theories explaining the workings of the universe at the time, was that there was a "life force" driving all creation. In fact, he conducted a number of discussions of the "true nature" of space and time with Albert Einstein, very much his contemporary, in which he presented an alternative approach built around a "life force" that he saw as driving all creation. Bergson's idea was that although the human mind is *predisposed* to perceive the universe as a static object in spatial juxtaposition and sees change as a succession of discrete changes in affairs, it was an illusion. The limitations of the "logical", mechanical universe approach have been set out clearly by such figures as the ancient philosopher Zeno with riddles of time and space (including the famous paradox of the race between Achilles and a tortoise, with the famous runner never being able to catch up to the tortoise).

Instead, for Bergson, the active, perceiving mind takes precedence. Time now does not consist of a present time but only of a hazily recollected past and an equally uncertain glimpse into the future. Words, too, give a misleading impression of stability and order to the world, which is "in reality" a shifting flux of fleeting sensations and experiences. And it is this promotion of intuition over intellect and unconscious thought logical method that jokes celebrate.

All of which points to why Bergson's third major work, *Laughter* (*Le Rire),* published in 1900, advocated humor as a way to escape the "prison" of words and concepts—a necessary task with an evangelical flavor that his

---

[41] Bergson 1912

earlier works on space and time had already identified. In 1914, an acknowledgement of sorts came from the Catholic Church, which was to put his books on its list of "banned" works! Alongside Galileo's musings on the solar system and fellow Frenchman Victor Hugo's *Hunchback of Notre Dame*. This last had been added to the index in 1834 because church censors found it to be "too sensual, libidinous, and lascivious."

Despite the celebrity being banned by Rome in the 1940s, Bergson was required, as a resident of Paris, to register as a Jew, and after queuing for many hours in the cold, he contracted pneumonia, from which he shortly after died. But perhaps the final indignity was that when the American philosopher, Charles Sanders Peirce, was compared to Bergson (by William James), Peirce felt himself maligned! But that's philosophers…they always want to claim their latest theory is unique to them.

That's said a little bit tongue-in-cheek, but Bergson's idea is that the special kind of thinking that we call humor is essentially social. The same thought is reflected in Wittgenstein's remark that 'the solitary man does not laugh' while Freud too has no doubt that we laugh, as he puts it, by ricochet. Freud recalls the words of Louis Dugas in the1902 book '*La Psychologie du Rire*':

'Laughter belongs to those manifestations of psychic states that are highly infectious; if I make someone else laugh by imparting my wit to him, I am really using him as a tool in order to arouse my own laughter.'[42]

This idea is a problem for a book like this. How funny can the jokes in it be when read privately and not shared? In my own experience, the answer is "less funny"…and yet certainly not entirely "unfunny". And after all, we can always read out the "best bits" of books to appreciative audiences. In such ways, jokes can take on a second life.

Joke #10: The Night Train

Two students, a man and a woman, who had never met before, found themselves in the same sleeping carriage of a train.

After the initial embarrassment and polite exchanges about where they have come from and where they are going, they both try to get to sleep, with the woman taking the top bunk, the man lying on the lower.

---

[42] Freud 1922, 242

In the middle of the night, the woman leans over and says, "I'm sorry to bother you, but I'm awfully cold, and I was wondering if you could possibly pass me another blanket."

The man looks in the cupboard under the bunk and sees that there are no more blankets. He climbs back into his bunk and explains the situation, adding, 'I've got another idea; let's pretend we're married!'

'Why not?' giggles the woman.

'So, just to be clear,' he replies.

'Keep your hands off my blanket.'

Chapter 3
The Comic Appeal of Humans as Machines

In this still from the film "Modern Times", Charlie Chaplin, playing a new factory employee, is splattered by the company's time-saving "Eating Machine" during his lunch break.

There's a scene in Charlie Chaplin's film, *Modern Times,* that makes Henri Bergson's theory about the humor of people being reduced to automata very well. It starts with Charlie happily working in the factory when the manager suddenly picks him to be the guinea pig for a new machine that is supposed to feed workers without them needing to stop work on the assembly line. (The film also makes a political point about humans being reduced to automata, of course.) So, an unsuspecting Charlie is strapped into the feeding machine.

At first, everything goes smoothly. A tray is lifted to the level of Charlie's face, and pieces of food are shoveled into his mouth by a mechanical arm. This is followed by a mounted cob of corn that slowly rotates between Charlie's parted teeth. Each feeding process is followed by the action of an automatic mouth wiper. It is at the soup course, however, that the machine starts to malfunction. Sparks start flying, and the soup is served on Charlie's shirt instead of to his mouth. As the machine's supervisor starts to try to correct it, the machine feeds nuts and bolts into Charlie's mouth. After he spits them out, the mouth wiper, out of control, keeps beating his head. Bigger sparks shoot out of the machine, whose movements become berserk.

The manager finally cancels the experiment and dismisses the inventor with the words, 'It's not practical', this being again, a comment on the "logic" of industrial automation. Because even if it had functioned as intended, it would have been morally offensive to reduce a human being merely to a cog in a machine. Machines repeat actions; humans do not.

Part of Chaplin's humor (as with other comedies of the silent films age) is the impassive expression that accompanies increasingly ridiculous events. The "stoneface" of a Chaplin, or Buster Keaton, or indeed the learned philosopher, Kant telling one of his long jokes at the dinner table, is as if 'the soul had allowed itself to be fascinated and hypnotized by the materiality of a simple action,' writes Bergson in his essay "Laughter: an Essay on the Meaning of the Comic," (which, recall, was published in 1900).[43] The comic behaves, in short, not as an autonomous individual but as a machine*. *The movements of the human body are laughable in exact proportion, as they remind us of a mere machine.* And the more exactly these two images—that of a person and that of a machine—fit into each other, the more striking the comic effect. It is "the illusion of a machine working on the inside of the person"

Curiously, the real Charlie Chaplin once entered a lookalike competition for Charlie Chaplins—and lost! Introducing himself afterwards to the surprised judges, Chaplin asked why they had felt he was inauthentic. The reason, they explained, was his blue eyes. The Charlie Chaplin in the films, of course, was only shades of gray.

Henri Bergson was writing his philosophy some years before silent films really took off, and instead uses facial expressions and caricatures as examples to develop another part of his "mechanical elasticity" argument. However, a phrase in his essay, on the confusion of human life and machines exactly sums up the humor of the Eating Machine:

---

[43] Bergson 1912, part III

'Any arrangement of acts and events is comic, which gives us, in a single combination, the illusion of life and the distinct impression of a mechanical arrangement.'[44]

In this short, but conceptually fertile, essay, Bergson also suggests that intuition is more important in understanding how people operate than rationality. He offers here, in Darwinian terms, that humor is a mechanism that has evolved to make social life possible for human beings. His favorite example is being a man slipping on a banana peel.

Okay, what's so funny about someone slipping on a banana skin. —as per a thousand clown routines or children's cartoons? Actually, I'm not sure that it is very funny, but the theory at least is clear—the banana skin upsets the decorous march of the clown or foils the frenzied dash of the villain. The humor lies in this failure of a planned routine—whether it be walking to work, or running from the cops, or eating while at the workplace—to cope with the unexpected circumstance.

Bergson calls the phenomenon "mechanical inelasticity" because human action has become mechanical, a planned sequence, and inelastic as the person is unable to respond to the new environment.

Let's widen the debate. Henri Bergson believes that everything gives a comic impression, which manifests itself in the shape of a machine-like, inanimate movement in the human being. His law is that 'the attitudes, gestures, and movements of the human body are laughable in exact proportion as that body reminds us of a mere machine.'[45] He explains the comic of imitation by connecting it with a problem formulated by Pascal in his *Thoughts*, why is it that we laugh at the comparison of two faces that are alike, although neither of them excites laughter by itself? 'The truth is that a really living life should never repeat itself. Wherever there is repetition or complete similarity, we always suspect some mechanism at work behind the living.'

However, as Freud points out, there are many cases of humans acting in a mechanical way that are not funny. Consider, he says, the motions made by a bowler after he has released the ball while he is following its course as though he were still able to control it, or the impassioned movements of a modern

---

[44] Bergson 1913, Part I
[45] Bergson 1913, Part V

orchestra leader, will appear comical to every unmusical person who cannot understand why they are necessary.

Imitating someone's gestures is comic; for this reason, repetition of all kinds provokes laughter. Consider a Punch and Judy show. The traditional, popular, and usually violent puppet show featuring Pulcinella (Mr. Punch) and his wife Judy and performed by a single puppeteer (known since Victorian times as a "professor", don't ask me why) inside a wooden booth. A third, and doubtless archetypal figure, is the policeman.

'We will now pass on to the theater, beginning with a Punch and Judy show. No sooner does the policeman put in an appearance on the stage than, naturally enough, he receives a blow that falls to him. As he springs to his feet, a second blow lays him flat. A repetition of the offense is followed by a repetition of the punishment. Up and down, the constable flops and hops with the uniform rhythm of the bending and release of a spring, while the spectators laugh louder and louder.'[46]

The scene presents something distinctly mechanical in puppets ostensibly living. Disentangle its central element, says Bergson, and we hit upon one of the core feature of comedy: *repetition*.

'The deflection of life toward the mechanical is here the real cause of laughter.'

The fact that Punch and Judy's protagonists are obviously puppets only adds to the appeal. For humans, too, are (and here Bergson recalls the words of the poet, René Sully Prudhomme):

'Humble marionettes/ The wires of which are pulled by fate.'

The humor lies in the fact that, as Bergson says, all that is serious in life comes from our freedom.

'The feelings we have matured, the passions we have brooded over, the actions we have weighed, decided upon, and carried through—in short, all that comes from us and is our very own—these are the things that give life its often dramatic and generally grave aspect. What, then, is the requisite to transform all this into a comedy? Merely to fancy that our seeming, freedom conceals the strings of a dancing-Jack.'[47]

---

[46] Bergson 1913, Part I
[47] Bergson 1913, Part VIII

We laugh when a small series of effects leads inexorably to something monstrous. We laugh when (equally inexorably) a saga unfolds, which brings the hero back to where they originally started. As Bergson says, we laugh—in fact, every time a person gives us the impression of being a thing. Just as Mr. Perrichon, on getting into the railway carriage, makes certain of not forgetting any of his parcels by carefully counting: 'Four, five, six, my wife seven, my daughter eight, and myself makes nine…'

Mr. Perrichon reduces himself to the status of an object. A worse error is made by a lady whom Cassini, the astronomer, had invited to see an eclipse of the moon. Arriving too late, she says, 'Monsieur de Cassini, I know, will have the goodness to begin it all over again, to please me.'

But Bergson's idea that comedy is the logic of the absurd goes much further. He writes that there is a logic of the imagination, which is not the logic of reason, something like the logic of dreams, 'though of dreams that have not been left to the whim of individual fancy, being the dreams dreamed by the whole of society.' In a joke, just as in a dream:

'A special kind of effort is needed, by which the outer crust of carefully stratified judgments and firmly established ideas will be lifted, and we shall behold in the depths of our mind, like a sheet of subterranean water, the flow of an unbroken stream of images that pass from one into another. This interpenetration of images does not come about by chance. It obeys laws, or rather habits, which hold the same relation to imagination that logic does to thought.'

'More than one philosophy of laughter revolves round a like idea. Every comic effect, it is said, implies contradiction in some of its aspects. What makes us laugh is alleged to be the absurd realized in concrete shape, a "palpable absurdity"; or, again, an apparent absurdity, which we swallow for the moment only to rectify it immediately afterwards; or, better still, something absurd from one point of view though capable of a natural explanation from another.'

(*Laughter: An Essay on the Meaning of the Comic*, Preface)

Certainly, the following little story is absurd. But there is a compelling logic to it. And the juxtaposition is pleasing.

Joke #11: A Little Old Lady Goes into the Bank

A little old lady goes to the bank with a handbag filled with $10,000 in cash and asks to open an account. The cautious banker asks where she got the money. 'Gambling,' she says. 'I'm very good at gambling.' Intrigued, the banker asks, 'What sort of bets do you make?'

'Oh, all sorts,' she says. 'For example, I would like to wager you $100 right now that by noon tomorrow you will have a dollar bill tattooed on your right buttock.' 'Well, I would love to take that bet,' chuckles the banker, 'but it wouldn't be right for me to take your money for such an absurd wager.' 'Let me put it to you this way,' says the woman. 'If you don't take the bet with me, I'll have to find another bank for my money.' 'Now, now, don't be hasty,' says the banker. 'I'll take your bet.'

The next day, the little old lady returns at noon, accompanied this time by an elderly lawyer, whom she says is there to act as a witness.

The banker shakes both their hands and then says, 'Well, I'm afraid we must test this lady's theory now!' He turns around, drops his pants, and invites the two to observe that he has won the bet.

'Fine,' says the woman, counting out the cash from her handbag. The lawyer, meanwhile, is sitting with his head in his hands.

'What's wrong with him?' asks the banker.

'Aw, he's just a sore loser,' she says.

'I bet him $10,000 that by noon today, you'd take your pants down to show us your buttocks in your office.'

Ho, ho, ho! But the story illustrates the point being made by Bergson very well.

'So, we see that absurdity, when met with in the comic, is not absurdity in general. It is an absurdity of a definite kind. It does not create the comic; rather, we might say that the comic infuses into it its own particular essence. It is not a cause but an effect—an effect of a very special kind that reflects the special nature of its cause.'[48]

To be humorous, there needs to be a thread of logic in the ridiculous. Or, as the French philosopher and novelist Albert Camus puts it in *The Myth of Sisyphus*, the absurd arises because the world fails to meet our demands for

---

[48] Bergson 1913, Part IV

meaning. Yet who are we to demand that the world make sense? For 'the absurdity of our situation derives not from a collision between our expectations and the world but from a collision within ourselves.'[49]

---

[49] *The Modern Psychologist*, n.d.

Chapter 4
Playing Games with the Laws of Cause and Effect

Jacques Lacan, the French psychoanalyst credited with reinterpreting Freud, was notoriously dull and obscure but hid little jokes in his lectures.

In everyday life, things become absurd if they seek to challenge nature's rules of cause and effect. It is "absurd" to wash the car when it is pouring with rain because the rain will wash the car anyway, and it is far worse to attempt to "dry" it. It is funny when you panic because one day the computer won't turn on, and then you realize you forgot to plug it in. Conversely, the rules structure our lives and make it possible to achieve our ends. If I heat the kettle, the water will boil, and tea can be made. The philosophical law that states:

If x then y
And x
Therefore: y

…is at the heart of logical reasoning. It offers a world in which we may not like what happens*, but at least there is order.* Sometimes, of course, the effect is undesirable. If I put the kettle on and then forget about it, to use the example of Agnes Heller in *The Immortal Comedy: The Comic Phenomenon in Art, Literature, and Life*, when I return in half an hour, the water will have disappeared and the kettle will be ruined too.

That's cause and effect carried on a little beyond the usual limits. A lot of jokes rely on simply pushing the "effect" a little bit further than the normal cause would allow. A more perplexing world, that upends the whole notion of 'conditional necessity' is nicely illustrated in this joke.

Joke #12: The Man on the Train to Odessa

A young man boarded a train bound for Odessa and found a carriage empty, except for a prosperous-looking passenger reading a newspaper. After some time, the young man leans forward and asks politely: 'Excuse me, sir, could you tell me the time?''

The other passenger angrily puts down his paper and glares at him. 'Absolutely not, and I resent your impudence! Get your own watch, wastrel!'

'What the devil is wrong with you!' the young man replies indignantly. 'I only asked you for the time!'

The other passenger makes it as though to continue reading his paper and then sighs and says, 'All right, I'll explain. First, would you like me to tell you the time, yes? But then there will be some small talk, and soon you will discover that we are both going to Odessa. Then it will turn out that we are both going to the International Arts Festival there, but that you do not have anywhere to stay, and all the hotels will be booked up. Inevitably, since I live in Odessa in a large house, I will have to invite you to stay there, in which case you will meet Sophie, my beautiful daughter. The likelihood is that the two of you will get on very well, and after a few more visits, you will both fall in love. At which point you will then expect my approval so that you and Sophie can get married. So now you wonder why I am angry. Because I refuse to let my daughter marry anyone who cannot even afford a watch!'

In the case of *The Man on the Train to Odessa*, the joke is that the supposed sequence of events is not really determined; at any point, there are too many other factors and indeed imponderables to make the assumption: 'the young man wants to have a big house and beautiful wife; therefore, he will try to marry my daughter' reliable. Yet once the absurd logic is accepted, the punchline itself does seem somehow reasonable, and this reasonable quality is also amusing in the contrast between the parochial nature of the concern and the grand events supposed to be linked. It is "chaos theory", the idea that a butterfly beating its wing in Brazil can, in so doing, trigger a cascade of ever-larger events that eventually finish in a hurricane in the United States.

By supposing that our lives and choices are predetermined and our freedom to act curtailed, the joke also makes concrete another problem with conditional necessity. Thomas Nagel has put it this way:

'Humans have the special capacity to step back and survey themselves and the lives to which they are committed, with that detached amazement that comes from watching an ant struggle up a heap of sand. Without developing the illusion that they are able to escape from their highly specific and idiosyncratic position, they can view it *as subspecies aeternitatis*—and the view is at once sobering and comical. We see ourselves from the outside, and all the contingency and specificity of our aims and pursuits become clear. Yet when we take this view and recognize what we do as arbitrary, it does not disengage us from life, and there lies our absurdity: not in the fact that such an external view can be taken of us, but in the fact that we ourselves can take it, without ceasing to be the persons whose ultimate concerns are so coolly regarded.'[50]

Commenting on this, writer and sometime priest Jonathan Clatworthy says each of us clings to the belief, or if not that, at least the hope that our lives have meaning. The fear that they have no meaning at all seemed to philosophers like Nietzsche and Sartre to have devastating implications, but for Thomas Nagel, like other more recent philosophers, the challenge is more about how to live in a godless universe apparently created without any plan. For Nagel, we have no choice but to live our lives as though they were *not* absurd. We can occasionally reflect philosophically on the fact that they are absurd, but then we must return to our familiar convictions 'with a certain irony and

---

[50] **Chapter 4:** Nagel 1971

resignation' as he puts it in his 1971 essay called simply "The Absurd". Unable to abandon the natural responses on which they depend, we take them back, 'like a spouse who has decided to run off with someone else and then decided to return,' but we regard them differently.

Indeed, the joke, despite being superficially trivial, points at several deep philosophical notions explored by existentialism. Just as another insight into the struggle for autonomy and authenticity (the two lodestones for the existentialist philosophers) comes from the following short tale.

Joke #13: The Man Who Thought He Was a Grain of Corn

A man is confined to a mental hospital because he sometimes has periods when he thinks he is a grain of wheat or corn. The doctors there tell him not to worry, as this kind of delusion is very common, and they are confident that after a series of sessions he can be cured.

Two years later, the man reports that the fears have departed, and the doctors announce that the cure is complete. The man is released from the hospital and walks out of the door into the open air when he immediately sees a pigeon. White-faced and clutching his head, he dashes back into the building and demands to see the chief psychiatrist.

The psychiatrist is puzzled because he was sure the delusion had been cured. He says to the man, 'Is there any doubt in your mind that you are not, in any sense, a grain of wheat or corn or anything like that?'

The man replies impatiently, 'Of course I know I'm not! The thing I'm worried about is…how does the pigeon know?'

Okay, so the man is still mad. That is in the joke. In real life, things are more complicated. As Michel Foucault puts it in his classic text, *Madness and Civilization* (published in 1964, and what a great year that was, too!)

'The man who imagines he is made of glass…thereby concludes that he is fragile, that he is in danger of breaking, that he must touch no object that might be too resistant, that he must in fact remain motionless, and so on. Such reasonings are those of a madman, but again, we must note that in themselves, they are neither absurd nor illogical. On the contrary, they apply correctly the most rigorous figures of logic. The ultimate language of madness is that of reason…'[51]

The Man Who Thought he was a Grain of Corn joke is known to have been a favorite of the "controversial" French psychiatrist, Jacques Lacan. Lacan was unashamedly dull and obscure; he famously counted money as a therapeutic technique, but like many dull philosophers that I know, he actually liked to hide little jokes in his long lectures. These were jokes people were not invited to laugh at, but rather jokes made to bolster their own sense of self-importance. For example, in a lecture about whether a pot of mustard depends on the word "mustard" on the pot for its essence, Lacan would stress in French the phrase, "ce condiment". The joke being (wait for it) the punning equivalence to *"ce qu'on dit ment"*, which in French means, 'that which I am saying is a lie.'

It seems that for Dr Lacan, this little play with words actually did quite a lot of conceptual heavy lifting, which is exactly what appealed to him about *The Man Who Thought he was a Grain of Corn* joke. Specifically, the joke illustrated nothing less than the relationship between 'the gaze of other people' in society and our own unconscious minds. The thing is that, for the man, it is not enough that he knows he is not a grain of corn; it is necessary to know what *other* people (or, in this case, birds) think. For Lacan, 'the Other who does not know' is actually our own unconsciousness.

Actually, the notion of "the Other" has a long philosophical pedigree— rather older than many continental philosophers seem to want to allow. For example, in the first half of the eighteenth century, Scotland's brilliant and consistently iconoclastic philosopher, David Hume, described himself as desperately trying to work out who exactly he was and finding that he was nothing more than a bundle of rapidly changing perceptions. Hume writes that:

'For my part, when I enter most intimately into what I call myself, I always stumble on some particular perception or other, of heat or cold, light or shade, love or hatred, pain or pleasure. I can never catch myself at any time without a perception, and I can never observe anything but the perception. When my perceptions are removed for any time, as by sound sleep, so long am I insensible of myself and may truly be said not to exist.'

– *A Treatise of Human Nature.* (Hume, 1738, Part 3, Section VI: Of Personal Identity)

---

[51] Foucault, 94

It is here that the 'gaze of the Other' comes in again, for good or ill. For bad, well, that's the pigeon looking at you. For good, it is more as that venerable English poet, Milton, put it when he wrote that everyone needs other people to have a good impression of themselves, or else they will become rotten, and that a 'pious and just honoring of ourselves' was 'the fountainhead whence every laudable and worthy enterprise issues forth.'[52]

Perhaps this is another way that jokes show their value in creating and protecting social life. Perhaps jokes help us to step back and see ourselves as we really are: fallible and human.

---

[52] Milton. 128

Chapter 5
Whatcha Gonna Do:
Pick a Goat or a New Car?

Pick a door! Behind a 20th century gameshow challenge lurked a surprisingly complex calculation.

Try this. You are on a game show, and there are three doors. The presenter, the famous Monty Hall, tells you that behind one of the doors there is a new car, and behind the other two are farmyard goats. If you pick the car, you win it. If you pick the goat, it is not clear what you will get, but it certainly won't be that car.

This is the so-called 'Monty Hall Problem,' once-upon-a-time a popular TV show, and still a very popular topic with philosophers. There are whole courses built around it! Because if it does not say so much about math, it does say something about psychology and, in particular, about the problems we all have coping with, "uncertainty". But first, the problem.

Working out which door to pick of three possibilities is just a matter of random chance and thus not very philosophical, let alone good TV. However, in the game show, Monty Hall, being a helpful sort of chap, adds a twist. After you have picked a door, he always opens a different door to reveal one of the two goats behind it. Then he gives you a chance to choose which of the other two doors you want to open.

Puzzle Number #1: Is Stick or Switch?

What should you do? Stick or switch? Stick with your original intuition or switch to the option Monty is nudging you toward. Or does it not really matter if the odds are 50/50?

In fact, you should switch. Contrary to what may seem intuitive, switching actually doubles the chances of winning the car. The gameshow fun highlights some quite serious truths about both pure mathematics and the logic of everyday life.

The key to understanding why the odds are not 50/50 at all, contrary to the promptings of fast-thinking "common sense", call it what you will, is that Monty knows the locations of the car and goats. His knowledge changes his actions and thus affects the odds.

Let me try to explain this baffling result. Most of us will consider the matter first by thinking about winning the car. From this perspective, it does seem, at the start of the game, that there is a one in three chance of picking up the door with the car behind it and that after Monty opens one of the "goat" doors, the odds improve—to evens. It's a two-door problem, not really complicated. There's the door you originally chose and one other. 50/50. That's how it seems, but appearances, as ever, can be deceptive, and sure enough, when you run actual games, it isn't 50/50 at all.

Why? Well, look at it instead from the point of view of the goats. (And changing your point of view is both what makes life entertaining and what brings insights.) At the beginning of the game, there is a 2:3 chance of selecting a door with a goat behind it. (Three doors, two goaty outcomes.) *So logically, it makes sense to assume your first guess was wrong. It's not sure if it's wrong, but it's simply much more likely—other things being equal—to have been wrong.* Now, when Monty opens one of the two remaining doors and reveals a goat, the odds of the last remaining door also concealing a goat are not fifty-fifty at all but instead significantly lower, about one in three. To put it short, the odds are that it is the car. But as I say, that is assuming your first guess was wrong. There's still a lingering sense in which "sticking" to your first choice and rejecting the door offered by Monty is quite "logical". Hence, the philosophical debate rumbles on in the academies. But really, it shouldn't, and indeed, if you're given a similar choice, you should reject intuition and go with the math. Or, if you like, go online to the site run by the University of California, San Diego where you can play the game and see which strategy works best in practice[53]. The site is a "real-life" experiment that records the fact that the odds really are overwhelmingly in favor of switching.

All of which goes to say that there is an answer to the Monty Hall Problem, 'which door to choose,' and even if it's not entirely a satisfactory one, it is a "seems to work" kind of one. So, given that there is a rather dull practical answer, why does the challenge—stick with your first intuition or take the host's challenge? have such appeal—beyond the eternal voyeuristic appeal of TV spectators watching people fail to win things? One answer is that Monty seems to like a conjuror who has goats and cars hidden, if not up his sleeve, behind his doors. For the audience,

The game is like a magic trick: our attention is diverted while a substitution is played.

And that is also why the Monty Hall Problem is a kind of joke, because in jokes, a similar kind of tricker, a similar kind of "substitution" goes on, again while our attention is distracted.

Another answer is surely that the problem involves things about preferring "our own" judgment to the advice of others—even on things when we really have no knowledge and no personal commitment to a particular position! In this sense, the critical thinker, the independently minded contestant, is likely to "stick" and lose.

There's another "mind twister" that offers a different perspective on the appeal of puzzle-solving in general. When it went "viral" on the internet not long ago, it stumped so many people that it became the stuff of serious newspaper reports concerning the current state of society. But it all seems harmless enough at first glance.

---

[53] **Visit** ucsd.edu

Puzzle Number #2: The Parking Space

The question is, what is the number of the parking space that the car is parked in?

If you can't work it out quickly, maybe try working it out slowly. But be assured, there really is an answer!

After wracking my brain for quite a few minutes, I got '78' as my answer. Actually, I was quite proud of that. I surmised that there had been a sequence of spaces numbered '6' which had then been followed by a sequence numbered '8,' with the ingenious bit of my explanation being that the painter had made an error and mixed up some of the spaces. Well, you know, it could happen in a busy city with lots of painting to be done.

My answer was, alas, wrong. The puzzle is very simple and simply requires—as with the Monty Hall goat challenge, as with all the best puzzles—a new angle on the problem. Think "outside the box" to find out what's inside the box.

In this case, try flipping the image around 180°. Now we realize that Henri Bergson had it right again: "The eye sees only what the mind is prepared to comprehend."

If you got it straight away, well, you'll be getting restless by now. But take it from me, most people get stuck (as I did), and this is why the puzzle is really worth its weight (although, admittedly, that's not very much) in gold. Why is it so hard sometimes to look at problems from a different perspective? Why do our minds seem designed to follow tramlines to disaster? Part of the answer is social: education consists largely of applying learned techniques to problems of similar kinds. If you tried to apply various math skills to this one, you reflect that social conditioning.

The image is a visual riddle because the essence of a riddle, as Aristotle remarked long ago, is to present the facts, but to do so in a puzzling way.

By comparison, here is a "word riddle", indeed perhaps THE original word riddle.

Puzzle Number #3: The Riddle of the Sphinx

What creature is it that walks on four legs in the early morning, two legs during the day, and three legs at dusk?

The riddle is supposed to have been demanded of all travelers on the road to Thebes by a sphinx, transplanted for no very obvious reason from her Ethiopian homeland to Greece. The rewards for getting the answer were not so great—merely to continue on the road—but the price of failure was to be eaten by the Great Cat. (A sphinx is literally a lion with a human head.)

Okay, the answer, in case you didn't know it, is coming up. One traveler, Odysseus, the hero of many Greek tales, quickly resolved the riddle with the answer "Man". A child crawls on all fours in its early years, walks on two feet for most of its life, and finally uses a stick as an additional "third leg" in old age. Thus, the riddle is merely about metaphors: a human life could be compared, metaphorically speaking, to a day, and a walking stick could be called a kind of leg.

Generalizing it, all riddles are an artful kind of wordplay, in which a more subtle relationship between things is revealed. This is why Aristotle praises riddles for playing tricks whose unmasking requires new insights:

"We have even more obviously learned something if things are the opposite of what we thought they were."—(Aristotle, *Rhetoric, 1412a*)

Actually, Aristotle, who is usually remembered for those rather dull explanations of grammatical and logical errors, was quite an admirer of the literary flourishes that appear as original metaphors or allegories. He says the ability to play with metaphors is the one "poetic ability" that cannot be either learned or taught.

'It is the mark of genius, for to make good metaphors implies an intuitive perception of similarities in dissimilar things.'—(*Poetics, Section 3, Part 23)*

And he adds, 'Good riddles do, in general, provide us with satisfactory metaphors; for metaphors imply riddles, and therefore a good riddle can furnish a good metaphor.'—(*Rhetoric,* Book III, Part III)

Another traditional riddle that perhaps Aristotle would have thought reveals the power of "word magic", is this one.

Puzzle Number #4: Who Calls?

What is it that hangs high up and cries out often to call its friends? It has a tongue in a large skull, but no hair. That has a long tail that reaches almost, but not quite, to the ground…?

The answer being…a church bell. All of these riddles play to a greater or lesser extent on certain ambiguities in language. One of the great literary demonstrations of the fun that can be had with that are the classic books *Alice in Wonderland* and *Alice through the Looking Glass*. These were both written in the 19th century by Lewis Carroll, the English writer, mathematician, logician, and keen amateur photographer. The books are, of course, nominally written for children—Carroll had a paternal friendship with a young girl called "Alice" who he hoped would enjoy the books—but in many ways, they are really a sophisticated collection of logical puzzles for mathematics and philosophers.

Jokes and "wit" more generally often involve the use of false logic, displacement, representation through the opposite, and many other varieties of absurdity, all of which appear in the works of Lewis Carroll. The mathematician understood, as Freud put it, that the "pleasure in nonsense" is 'in the seriousness of our lives, crowded back almost to the vanishing point.'

Part of the reason for this is that philosophers, ever since Schopenhauer, have sought to disparage such things. Schopenhauer, a century earlier, had identified not only obscene jokes but all jokes that play with words as a spurious kind of wit, writing:

"…the play upon words, the *calembourg*, the pun, to which may be added the equivocation, the double entendre, the chief use of which is the expression of what is obscene." (Schopenhauer 79)

Schopenhauer goes on to complain of a "miserable mania" prevailing in Germany during his time "for giving things a more distinguished name than belongs to them". Thus, he protests, every public house is called a hotel, every moneychanger is a banker, and every clown or joker is a humorist. Schopenhauer protests that this should be resisted, for "the word humor is borrowed from the English in order to single out and denote a quite peculiar species of the ludicrous, which is even akin to the sublime. [I]t is not meant to be used as a title for any jest or buffoonery." [54]

Schopenhauer and Carroll, we might say, would *not* have gotten on well together at a party.

Carroll's kind of humor is both logical and mathematical and yet, at the same time, a return to an earlier, more innocent kind of childish humor, a simple pleasure in wordplay. Put another way, Carroll's wordplay allows him to return to reconnecting with childhood freedoms, just as Freud says wit, more generally, does. Freud adds that older children, let alone adults, lose this freedom to enjoy life, to simply play, prevented by a kind of logic of real life, but through his *Alice* books, Carroll introduced many to a newly recovered space built around an inverted logic of the absurd.

Consider, for example, *nothingness*. The terror of growing up for children and adults alike has become a plaything. For example, as part of Alice's introduction to power, the Red Queen urges Alice to consider the peculiar properties of subtraction, starting by asking what would remain if you took a bone away from a dog.

Having considered this question carefully, Alice replies:

'The bone wouldn't remain, of course, if I took it—and the dog wouldn't remain; it would come to bite me—and I'm sure I shouldn't remain!'

'Then you think nothing would remain?' said the Red Queen.

'I think that's the answer.'

'Wrong, as usual,' said the Red Queen. 'The dog's temper would remain.'

'But I don't see how…'

'Why, look here!' The Red Queen cried. 'The dog would lose its temper, wouldn't it?'

'Perhaps it would,' Alice replied cautiously.

'Then if the dog went away, its temper would remain!' the Queen exclaimed triumphantly.'[55]

Likewise, as part of a discussion of birthday presents, Humpty Dumpty informs Alice that 'there are three hundred and sixty-four days when you might get un-birthday presents,' while wandering through Wonderland, Alice meets nobody on the road, leading the Red King to remark admiringly: 'To be able to see Nobody! And at that distance, too!'

---

[54] Schopenhauer II, 101

[55] Carroll, Chapter IX

In the jargon of the philosophy of language, to treat "nothing" and "nobody" as noun phrases (phrases that lead with a noun—a person, place, or thing) is to give properties to, well, non-existent entities. Some argue that a similar mistake to that of the Red King is made with terms like "mind" and "soul" it is easy enough to say, for example, that we have a soul, and then to argue about whether or not it survives after death, without realizing that the words used may be misleading us.

Carroll, a scholar of classical Greece, was fascinated by the power of Nothingness, and knew that Homer too played with the concept. In one of the best-known Greek myths, the dashing hero Odysseus uses a cunning trick to outwit the one-eyed giant Cyclops. By telling Cyclops that his own name is "Nobody", he leads the drunken monster to shout out uselessly at the critical moment: 'Nobody is killing me by treachery!'

Well, maybe it works better in the original Greek…

But consider another, more contemporary, joke that also plays with the concept of nothingness.

Joke #14: Happiness or a Ham Sandwich?

Suppose that you are a young actress newly arrived in Hollywood. All you really want in life is to be a famous, rich film star. So, which is better, to be the star of a Hollywood blockbuster or to get a bit of a part in a cornflake advertisement? It would appear that being a film star is the better outcome, but this is really not so!

Consider the matter more logically…

Clearly, for you, nothing could be better than being the star of a Hollywood blockbuster, yet a bit of a part in a cornflake advertisement is certainly better than…nothing.

Therefore, logically and like it or not, the bit part in the advert is better than the leading role in the blockbuster.

Now you know why so many aspiring hopefuls who go to Hollywood end up just doing crummy jobs…Formally, it looks like an argument with two premises and a conclusion that really ought to follow:

Lions are bigger than cats.

Elephants are bigger than lions.

Therefore, elephants are bigger than cats.

So far, so uncontroversial. In this case, though, we have something that, although it seems to have the same logical structure, the conclusion is much less persuasive.

Nothing is better than being the star of a Hollywood blockbuster.

A bit of a part in an advertisement is *better than nothing.*

Therefore:

A small part in an advertisement is better than being the star of a Hollywood blockbuster.

There are many versions of the "paradox", but personally, what I like about it is that it echoes the very real confusions concerning existential (life-changing) choices we all make—and often wonder why later. Investigating our choices, how we make them, and where we go wrong, is the subject of the next chapter.

At one level, it's just a play on the word "nothing" really; as discussed in the following little joke, it's always popular with philosophers, called 'Sartre Orders a Coffee.'

Joke #15: Sartre Orders a Coffee...

A man is sitting at a French cafe, reading (or at least pretending to) a long, complicated philosophy book. After a while, the waitress comes over to take his order. He orders a cup of coffee with no cream. The waitress disappears for a minute and then returns apologetically, 'I'm sorry, Monsieur, but we're out of cream. Will a coffee with no milk do instead?'

The joke, for students of philosophy anyway, is that in his long, windy book *Being and Nothingness*, the 20th century writer and philosopher, Jean-Paul Sartre, insists that: 'an absence of something is still something.'

Thus, there really is a difference between the cup of coffee with 'no cream'—and the cup of coffee with no milk. Or is there? In fact, for all that such wordplay seems trivial, there are real issues lurking. Profound? Important? I wouldn't say so necessarily…But philosophical insights, as Pierro Sraffa's gesture to Wittgenstein (mentioned in chapter one) illustrates, can come from far less.

Chapter 6
Stand-up Comedians as Today's Ethics Busters

Henrik Fladseth performing at the "aptly named",
Crap Comedy Festival in Oslo in January 2016.

Here's a joke that brings back not-so-fond memories of my own school days.

Joke #16: The Classroom

Teacher: Everyone who thinks they are stupid, stand up.

The class sits silently, heads bowed in shame. After a while, one boy, Johnny, slowly stands up.

Teacher: Ah, so we have one stupid person among us!

Johnny: It's not that, ma'am. Actually, it broke my heart to see you standing there alone.

Perhaps the thing that makes this joke work is that we can all recognize the drama of standing up in front of the class. Which brings me to the very real drama of stand-up comedy. This is significantly different from telling jokes to friends, let alone sharing jokes anonymously in the form of magazines or books, like this one. No, the stand-up comedian is engaged in a battle with the audience, hence the language of "dying" on stage. Stand-up comedy is a strange kind of battle in which either the audience or the comedian must be humiliated at the end. All of which helps explain why stand-up comics see jokes as being all about breaking taboos.

Many stand-up comedians have had brushes with the law. Fifties hepcat and stand-up trailblazer Lenny Bruce was repeatedly arrested and tried for obscenity, or in the words of his prosecutor during a 1964 trial, for 'nauseating word pictures...spewed directly at the audience.'[56] Recalling his career, Jay Rayner quipped in *The Observer* that 'Bruce could be very dirty, although not in any way that could ever be helped by soap.' (*The Observer,* 1999) Without doubt, though, Bruce was the inspiration for many modern comedy clubs. As Rayner says, 'He talked about the kind of stuff that makes you slam back in your seat, rigid with shock, horror, and surprise. He talked about loveless couples who found a bond through their shared bout of venereal disease. He did material about white liberals entertaining 'their colored friends.''

For Kenneth Tynan, *The Guardian*'s drama critic in the sixties, the real message of Bruce's routine was that he wanted us to be shocked, but by the right things.' 'Not by four-letter words, which violate only convention, but by want and deprivation, which violate human dignity.'[57]

And so, for a certain kind of liberal, the rudeness and edginess of Bruce have a heroic quality—even dare I say, a Christian quality? Because Bruce was found guilty and died of a drug overdose while on parole, pending his appeal against charges of obscenity.

Yes, it's a ridiculous, perhaps offensive comparison, but guess what? At the end of the 1990s, posters advertising a play about Bruce, portrayed by the

---

[56] **Chapter 6**: LennyBruce.org)
[57] In the Sunday edition, *The Observer,* 1999

contemporary comic Eddie Izzard, proclaimed him 'the Jesus Christ of stand-up,' who. 'Died so alternative comedy could live.'

Magnificent though Bruce's sacrifice was, the path to comedic free speech in the last century was a pretty bumpy one.

Bruce's fellow US comic, George Carlin, had a riff about rude words that actually led to a legal fight between the Federal Communications Commission (FCC) and a radio broadcaster that aired the routine—a case that went to the Supreme Court.

Originally, the "Feds" (the FCC) characterized the language of the monologue, which depicted sexual and excretory activities in a particularly offensive manner, as "indecent" and "patently offensive", though not obscene, and ruled it should be regulated by principles analogous to "law of nuisance" wherein the 'law generally speaks to channeling behavior rather than actually prohibiting it.'[58]

Under the US principles of free speech, being "offensive" is not an offense, if you see what I mean, but indecency frequently is. The British went through this process in the 1950s with that very literary work, *Lady Chatterley's Lover*, deemed unfit for public consumption in the United States, Canada, Australia, India, and Japan—and probably elsewhere too. Recall that, at this time, the arguments in Britain hinged on a legal test of "obscenity", which was broadly targeted by a new law, the 1959 Obscene Publications Act, which however allowed an exception for 'works of literary merit.' The trial became a major public event, and with the prosecution citing the book's repeated use of rude words—yes, the F-one and the C-one too, and famously asking the jury to ask themselves whether it was the kind of book 'you would wish your wife or servants to read,'[59] sending political progressives everywhere apoplectic. Eventually, however, it was the English gentry choking on their cornflakes when the verdict, delivered on 2 November 1960, came in as "not guilty." The ruling led to a far greater degree of freedom to publish explicit material in the United Kingdom.

But back to the US, where social conservatism still rules in many places. And although the Court of Appeal reversed the federal commission's finding as an infringement of the right to freedom of speech, the elderly judges of the

---

[58] FindLaw.com, no date
[59] Rolph 1961, page x

Supreme Court then weighed in, saying that yes, the Constitution protects free speech, but that certain kinds of speech were not worthy of protection![60]

All of this explains why 'FCC v. Pacifica,' in 1978, became a standard case to teach in law schools. As George Carlin recalled later in his autobiography, 'I take perverse pride in that. I'm actually a footnote to the judicial history of America.'[61]

It also explains why, as Brian Logan wrote in *The Guardian* (28 June, 2022), stand-up comedy continues to be something of the front-line in an ongoing war between defenders of free speech, however unpleasant, and self-appointed guardians of public morals.

You have to feel a bit sorry for the stand-up comedian trying to earn a crust in a dingy nightclub. Newspapers and publishers have posh lawyers checking their articles and manuscripts, but no one is there to protect stand-ups.

In 2010, for example, after Canadian stand-up Mike Ward made fun of the child singer Jérémy Gabriel, who has Treacher Collins syndrome, which can affect facial bone structure and cause deafness, the singer's family filed a human rights complaint, and Ward lost. The skit led to eleven years of litigation, until eventually, in 2021, Canada's Supreme Court ruled in the comedian's favor, judging his routine to be "nasty and disgraceful" but not illegal.[62]

A slightly less grudging victory for comics came in the US after would-be senator Roy Moore's campaign was dogged by allegations of sexual misconduct with teenagers. Moore sued Sacha Baron Cohen after the comedian, in his TV show *Who Is America?* used a fake pedophile detector on him as part of a supposed interview on US-Israel relations, with the legally actionable part of the skit being that the fake detector beeped. The lawsuit was dismissed by a judge, who described the segment as "clearly a joke."[63]

I doubt if the judge would have been familiar with quite what that four-letter word, "joke", actually brings with it. But we can look a bit deeper. Freud divides jokes into two very different kinds. There are "innocent" jokes, where the joke is a kind of escape from normal rules and the adult world, and there are what he dubs "tendentious jokes", where the joke allows space for

---

[60] Supreme Court Advance Decisions Volume 60, 365

[61] ConstitutionCenter.org

[62] RCI 2021

[63] *The Guardian*, 7 July 2022

suppressed aggression or resentment. Freud says that these jokes are the ones that lead to the loudest laughter! Essentially, the function of tendentious jokes is to create a socially acceptable space for thoughts that are otherwise socially unacceptable. It is the sense of release from suppressed feelings of aggression toward others that provides the enjoyment. At the same time, of course, such jokes also reveal aggression or inadequacy on the part of the people laughing at them or the person telling them.

Pause, if you will, for a moment to consider what this word "tendentious", which appears some 48 times in the English translation by James Strachey, *signifies*—to follow a strategy that, indeed, Freud regularly asks us to use for all kinds of other things,

The word "tendentious" in English actually comes from German. To be precise, it arrived in the English language in 1871, having come originally from the medieval Latin word *tendentia,* meaning "tendency". However, James Strachey adds a footnote explaining that while the German substantive *tendenz* is throughout the book translated "purpose", the German adjective derived from it, *tendenziosd,* is directly rendered as "tendentious" in the sense of "representing facts in a partisan manner, often manipulatively so".

Additionally, in English, the word means expressing or intending to promote a particular cause or point of view, especially a controversial one.

But the core point is that when jokes are "tendentious", it means they *attack* something—though the target might, in Freud's view, be something as impersonal as "logic", a qualification that means that effectively all and any jokes that play with normal rules can be called tendentious. Indeed, Freud further undermines his own distinction, as he says that all jokes allow us to escape the rules of thinking and speaking and, in this way, to "renounce" our social commitments.

And now to the actual practice. Tendentious jokes in action. I mentioned Chris Rock in the introduction, the New York comic whose trademark is precisely to be "unexpected". But in an interview with Christopher John Farley for *Time Magazine*[64], he goes into a bit more detail, saying, 'Somebody should always be offended. Somebody in your life should always be like, *Why did you have to do that?* Always. That's just being a real artist. That's the difference between Scorsese and Disney.'

---

[64] *Time* 1999

So, what do these convention-busting jokes look like? In his early days, his trademark joke was this, 'Woman comes up to me and says she'll do anything for me, anything. So I say, "Bitch, paint my house!"' Rock launched his career, basically, with this joke. Maybe you've got to see the whole show maybe drink a bit to really appreciate it. But for Farley, 'The material was angry, real, and so funny it hurt.'

Or was it maybe more like Jerry Seinfeld, a pal of Rock's, says—in response to Farley's admiring query about Rock's 'hip-hopping in-your-face style.' Seinfield replied, 'It's the yelling that makes it special. It's very easy to hear what he's saying. Beyond that, I don't see anything special about it.' Funny or bitchy? It's a fine line—in life as well as on the comedy circuit. Farley, though, is sure that "among comics", such joking put-downs 'are the ultimate display of *respect*.'

Or listen to Cody Woods, a Los Angeles-based comic who has direct experience of the cold reality of life as a stand-up. He says the material for the routines has changed as society itself has moved on. Today's comics are less interested in jokes about mothers-in-laws and wives, as most of the audience are not in conventional marriages anyway. On the other hand, what Woods calls "social justice" material is becoming more and more common, although he says most of it is not very funny.

'Go to any bar show in NYC or LA and take a shot anytime you hear: Trump, gentrification, white privilege, dating, online dating, Trump, fuckboys, feminism, police brutality, prejudice, Trump, Trump, mansplaining, dick pics, Trump and Trump, anxiety, nerdy stuff and Trump.'[65]

It's so unfunny; chances are, 'You'll be dead halfway through the show,' Woods says disloyally, adding that it's not even that comedy was any more original in the days of yore. In fact, there's a lot of familiarity with the routines once the topical veneer is removed. Themes like 'Men versus women, Airplane food, how annoying a spouse is, what it was like "back then," and finally, have you ever noticed this observation that I have noticed?'

Woods says that comedians think they are original (who doesn't?). But in actual fact, not only is the material largely copperplate, but even the delivery is. Although, on this, he thinks there are fashions, and at the moment the fashion is away from the rapid scatter-fire style of the last century to a more

---

[65] Quora.com

laid-back "ironic" style to the extent that some of today's stand-up comedy 'sounds more like a TED talk or therapy session' than comedy.

Did someone say therapy? But yes, the great unexpected truth about comedy clubs is that they are a form of psychotherapy, and by the same count, they must also be about human ethics.

In both ways, they are part of a long tradition. For the father of psychoanalysis, Sigmund Freud, too, humor is merely the device used by the unconscious mind to evade the restrictions imposed on it by the conscious. Laughter is essentially a release of excess energy. Where does this energy come from? From the temporary lifting of inhibition.

This is what comedy clubs are really all about. The exotic venue, the alcohol, the low lights, the anonymity…just as much as the vulgarity and the swearing, it all says, 'Here, normal rules do not apply.'

Freud explains all this in his careful, scholarly studies. Keeping down forbidden impulses, he says, requires an expenditure of psychic effort. When the cunning devices of a joke force such a thought or feeling to be entertained (by presenting it in an outwardly innocent guise), the energy used to maintain the inhibition against it is released.

In his classic work, *Jokes and their Relationship to the Unconscious*, Freud arrived at the following conclusion:

'Economy in the expenditure of inhibitions or suppressions, seems to be the secret of the pleasurable effect of tendency wit,'[66]

Adding that "the euphoria we are striving to obtain" is a return to a childhood time when we did not need humor to make us happy and "wit makes use of a means of connection which is rejected by and carefully avoided in serious thinking"[67]. (Which is why a joke explained is never funny.) Instead, for Freud, jokes and dreams share a common origin in the unconscious and are both essentially means of outwitting the inner 'censor.'

Yet there is a critical difference, he adds. Jokes have to be understood; indeed, this is crucial to their success. Dreams, by contrast, remain unintelligible—even to the dreamer—and are therefore totally uninteresting to other people. In a sense, *a dream is a failed joke.*

For Freud, jokes, like dreams, employ indirect experiences and allusions. 'Representation through the opposite is so common in dreams that even the

---

[66] Freud 1922, 180
[67] Freud 1922, 182

popular but entirely misleading books on dream interpretation usually put it to good account. Indirect expression, the substitution for the dream thought by an allusion, by a trifle, or by a symbolism analogous to comparison, is just exactly what distinguishes the manner of expression of the dream from our waking thoughts. Such a far-reaching agreement as found between the means of wit-work and those of dream-work can scarcely be accidental.'[68]

Consider this story that plays gently with an everyday social taboo, that I've lightly adapted from the version in a book called *Too Good to Be True: The Colossal Book of Urban Legends*[69]. Urban legends are similar to jokes in that they have a certain structure, yet each bit of the legend is negotiable; the ultimate criterion is the entertainment value!

Joke #17: A Woman Goes into a Railway Buffet

A woman goes into a railway buffet and buys a coffee, a newspaper, and (because she's peckish) a cheese platter consisting of cheese, butter, and crackers. All the tables are occupied, so she puts her purchases on the table and sits down opposite a respectable looking businessman. The woman sips her coffee and acknowledges a faint nod from the businessman.

Imagine the scene then: two smart travelers in a public railway buffet taking a coffee before their trains. It doesn't look like the kind of place where anything weird could happen, but on this day, it certainly did. The businessman leaned across the table, took the plate with the cheese and crackers on it, and peeled the covering off it. He then opens the crackers, unwraps the foil around the little packet of butter, and slowly butters one of the crackers. Then, he slices a piece of the cheese. Place it on the cracker and nonchalantly chomp the whole thing while at the same time reading his paper. The extraordinary thing about this surreal scene was the way he behaved, as if what he was doing was the most natural thing in the world.

The situation was so outrageous and so unexpected that it seemed somewhat hard to deal with. What was a woman to do? In America, she could have brought out a small lady pistol and shot him. But this was in England, and such things are not done. Yet to say, 'Excuse me, but I bought those crackers for myself' seemed somehow not to rise to the issue. Add to which there was

---

[68] Freud 1922 126
[69] Brunvand 2011, page 30 "The Package of Cookies"

something so mad about the whole thing that the situation seemed rather threatening. And yet, the woman had bought the crackers for herself, and she was peckish. So, what she did was this. She gave the man a hard look and deliberately reached across the table, took the plate with the half-eaten packet of crackers, and pulled it over in front of her. She then slowly buttered a cracker for herself and chopped another slice of cheese, while the businessman watched her intently the whole time from behind his paper.

For a few moments, she began to relax and thought to herself, 'Well, that showed him!' But evidently it hadn't, because the man again lowered his paper, reached back across the table, pulled back the plate, and started repeating the process on the third of the four crackers.

For the woman, having said nothing the first time, it seemed somehow feeble to mention it now. So instead, the whole process repeated itself: she leant across the table, pulled the plate back to her area of the table, took out the last cracker, buttered it, took the last bit of cheese, and quickly munched through it, ignoring the man's stares.

Who knows what might have happened, but fortunately, at that moment, the man's train was announced, and he put down his drink, got up, and without a word, headed out of the door.

The woman finished her coffee with quiet satisfaction at the way she had handled the impasse, and then when her train was announced, she stood up and picked up her paper. *Underneath it, neatly sealed and untouched was another, identical plate of cheese and crackers. The one she had bought earlier.*

I don't know if such a thing ever really happened to anyone. The joke is something of an "urban legend", attributed variously (I think wrongly) to Douglas Adams, a church minister from West Virginia. Whatever. There are many variations of it, and surely many social situations rest on such simple errors. Errors, not of reasoning exactly, as in the all-important starting assumptions. The story illustrates the way in which, far from conventional detective wisdom, it is the details that mislead. The whole thing is again like a magic trick: our attention is focused on these extraordinary and persuasive details while the 'switch' (in this case, literally a switch between two plates of cheese and crackers) goes unremarked.

This story certainly illustrates the idea that humor lies in a sudden shift of perspective, as well as perhaps here offering a warning against assumptions based upon appearances.

The same point is made in this very simple joke.

Joke #18: Attitudinal Problems

A man is driving down a narrow country road. A woman is driving up the same road. They pass each other very close.

The woman yells out her window, 'Pig!'

The man shouts back, 'Bitch!'

The man rounds the next curve, comes immediately across a large, speckled pig dozing in the middle of the road, skids, and crashes off the road and into a tree!

The famous 20th century philosopher Ludwig Wittgenstein's comment (that started this book off) that humor 'is not a mood but a way of looking at the world,' finds an echo here. In this case, yes, you really should be more charitable in your assumptions about other people. The joke is moralizing in a positive way, which contradicts the claim that humor lies in undermining social conventions and standards. Henri Bergson's analysis is more to the point: he says that in laughter we always find an undeclared intention to humiliate and consequently to correct our neighbor, if not in his will, at least in his deed, and that it is for this reason that a comedy is far more like real life than a drama is.

'It is the faults of others that make us laugh, provided we add that they make us laugh by reason of their *unsociability* rather than of their *immorality*.'[70]

The joke also includes that characteristic 'sudden shift in understandings' that Thomas Cathcart and Daniel Klein have suggested is the hallmark of humor. But it also contains a hint that we need to change the way we look at the world more generally too.

Other jokes are, frankly, unethical. Perhaps surprisingly, the 'master of suspense,' Alfred Hitchcock, whose films in a sense entertained so many, also perverted his abilities into unpleasant practical jokes. Hitchcock's films, featuring creepy scenes involving birds suddenly attacking cyclists (and hey,

---

[70] Bergson 1912, Chapter III, Part I

that's really happened to me!) or women being stabbed in showers, rely on the filmmaker's talent for getting inside people's heads and playing with their deepest fears. On the silver screen, okay. You can hide behind the sofa if you need to. Unfortunately, Hitchcock did not restrict his talent to this because, as he once admitted[71] to fellow film director Francois Truffaut, he had:

"…a weakness for practical jokes and have played quite a few in my time."

The pranks varied from more-or-less harmless japes, through mind games typical of the 'master of suspense,' and on to sadistic humiliation. Indisputably, some of his victims were hurt by his jokes, though. One case in particular was widely condemned as "unfunny" and had an effect on his reputation. In a 1983 biography of Hitchcock, *The Dark Side of Genius*, written by Donald Spoto, the following tale is recalled:

Hitchcock bet the film's property man a week's salary that he would be too frightened to spend a whole night chained to a camera in a deserted and darkened studio.

The chap heartily agreed to the wager, and at the end of the assigned day, Hitchcock himself clasped the handcuffs and pocketed the key—but not before he offered a generous beaker of brandy 'the better to ensure a quick and deep sleep.' The man thanked him for his thoughtfulness and drank the brandy, and everyone withdrew.[72]

When they arrived on the set the next morning, they found the poor man angry, weeping, exhausted, and humiliated. Hitchcock had laced the brandy with the strongest available laxative, and the victim had, unavoidably, soiled himself and a wide area around his feet and the camera.'

The "joke" doesn't work for me either as an imaginary story or an actual practical trick. But Hitchcock's joke would certainly have been recognizable as such to those who base humor on a "loss of control". In classical texts, great hilarity is found in tales of men who would like to be fighting the Spartans but instead are walking around with 'erect phalluses because their wives deny them sex' (ho ho ho), while a farmer who wants to study alongside the philosophers is unable to stop farting because he has eaten a lot of bean soup…In texts like the so-called "Old Comedy" of Aristophanes, actual human tragedies are considered to contain a comic element if they include this sense of a loss of control (especially by grand figures) over events.

_____

[71] *The Telegraph*, 2016
[72] Spoto, page 121

Henri Bergson, himself a very moral man, nonetheless appreciated humor's role in releasing us from our moral codes. Jokers, he says, are allowed to abandon social convention, just as they are allowed to abandon logic. 'Here, too, our first impulse is to accept the invitation to take it easy,' says Bergson. 'For a short time, at all events, we join in the game. And that relieves us from the strain of living.'[73] But inherent in the approach is that laughter, being directed at humiliation, must make a painful impression on the person against whom it is directed.

Freud theorizes the following: 'The pleasure of wit originated from an economy of expenditure in inhibition, or the comic from an economy of expenditure in thought, and of humor from an economy of expenditure in feeling.'

Humor is a means of obtaining pleasure despite the distressing effects that interfere with it; it acts as a substitute for the generation of these effects; it puts itself in their place. If we are in a situation that tempts us to release painful effects according to our habits and motives and then urges us to suppress these effects *in statu nascendi*, we have the conditions for humor.

In the cases just cited, the person affected by misfortune, pain, *etc.* could obtain humorous pleasure while the disinterested party laughs over the comic pleasure.

And Freud goes on:

'Wit permits us to make our enemy ridiculous through that which we could not utter loudly or consciously on account of existing hindrances; in other words, wit affords us the means of surmounting restrictions and of opening up otherwise inaccessible pleasure sources.'[74]

On the other hand, wit can pluck the sting from aggression and hostility too. If sexual references make for dangerous jokes, what of crudely racist ones? Freud recalls the example of Wendell Phillips, set out in what was then a recent biography, by Dr. Lorenzo Sears. Phillips, apparently, was on one occasion lecturing in Ohio, and while on a railroad journey to keep one of his appointments met with a number of clergymen who were returning from some sort of convention.

One of the ministers, feeling called upon to approach Mr. Phillips, asked him, 'Are you Mr. Phillips?'

---

[73] Bergson, chapter 3 part V
[74] Freud 1922, 150

'I am, sir.'

'Are you trying to free the niggers?'

'Yes, sir; I am an abolitionist.'

'Well, why do you preach your doctrines up here? Why don't you go over to Kentucky?'

'Excuse me, are you a preacher?'

'1 am, sir.'

'Are you trying to save souls from hell?'

'Yes, sir, that's my business.'

'Well, why don't you go there?'[75]

Freud notes that in view of the witty rejoinder, we are inclined to forget that the aggressor's inquiry itself was intended to be witty.

Of course, most jokes are just imaginary, and their breaches of ethics are very gentle. Take this one about a little boy who wants a new bike.

Joke #19: The New Bicycle

A young boy used to pray every night for a new bicycle. Nothing ever arrived, though, no matter how devoutly he prayed. Slowly, he realized that God doesn't work that way and changed his approach. Sure enough, one day he came across a fine bicycle locked to a lamppost outside the local library. So, he got a hacksaw and stole it, and later that night he prayed to the Lord for forgiveness.

That's alright, because, well, it's only a joke. Oh, oh…how often have bullies and sociopaths said that? There's got to be a line drawn somewhere. In the New Bicycle joke, it is devout folk who get a little poke, while poor people have a chuckle. So, I think it's all right. But that's only me, and without a doubt, for most of history, humor has been firmly in the service of the powerful. It's a tradition that goes right back to the dawn of recorded history, in Ancient China, where it seems that the Chinese were the first comics, as they were first in many other things. The first to invent paper; the first to invent gunpowder; and now the first to invent jokes! At least, that is, as far as the evidence of written texts goes. From these, we see that Lao Tzu, Chuang Tzu, and even Confucius were quite witty in their own ways.

---

[75] Freud 1922, 151

That said, Confucius did also, apparently, order the execution of several comedians after they had performed for the Dukes Qi and King Lu in Narrow Valley in 500 BCE. It seems he felt that their jokes involved insulting their betters. This action established what the Chinese call The Narrow Valley principle, which basically is that humor should serve socially desirable functions in general and reinforce respect for the authorities in particular. For thousands of years, the Chinese have struggled as a result with the reality that socially useful jokes are really not very funny. On the contrary, laughter's social purpose is much more, as Henri Bergson says, to neutralize the arrogance and conceit that otherwise sap social cohesion.

That laughter is profoundly social is shown by the way that it occurs almost uniquely in social settings. 'Laughter appears to stand in need of an echo' says Henri Bergson.

'Listen to it carefully: it is not an articulate, clear, well-defined sound; it is something that would fain be prolonged by reverberating from one to another, something beginning with a crash, to continue in successive rumblings, like thunder in a mountain. Still, this reverberation cannot go on forever. It can travel within as wide a circle as you please; the circle remains, none the less, a closed one. Our laughter is always the laughter of a group.'[76]

To understand laughter, Bergson insists, we must put it back into its natural environment, which is society, and above all, 'We must determine the utility of its function, which is a social one…Laughter must answer certain requirements of life in common. It must have a social signification.'

Nonetheless, where the Chinese rulers led, the European philosophers followed. The ancient Greeks largely accepted this Chinese disapproval of the jokers. Plato (427–348 B.C.) saw humor as opposed to sound reasoning to the extent that, although there are many jokes scattered in the conversations, out of all his many dialogues, Socrates himself is only allowed one eeny-weeny expression of merriment as part of the *Phaedo* dialogue—the one that is all about his preparations for death. As Socrates is allowed just this one funny line, I should record it properly. The joke starts when he is in his room drinking the cup of hemlock that the Athens court has ordered him to sip as the penalty for insulting the gods and leading young people astray—both offenses that comedians will feel are the least they should be doing, of course. Anyway, in

---

[76] Bergson, chapter I, part I

the rather drawn-out scene, his friends are with him and ask, 'But how shall we bury you?' and he replies.

'However, you please, if you can catch me and I do not get away from you!' And he laughed gently, and looking toward us, he said, 'I cannot persuade Crito, my friends, that the Socrates who is now conversing and arranging the details of his argument is really the one whom he will presently see as a corpse.'

(*Phaedo,* 115b)

For the philosophers of humor, Plato's keynote is to highlight "self-deception" as the essence of comedy. Apart from this bit of levity, though, Socrates seems to be resolutely opposed to the tricks and deceptions that humor usually consists of.

Today, jokes and laughter are so firmly entrenched in our minds as "good things", that it can be hard to really relate to how most of the ancient philosophers saw jokes—and after all, there were also ancients who used humor in a profoundly modern way even back then. We tend to see jokes through rose-tinted glasses and offer jokers the benefit of the doubt in cases where offense may be caused. But few would go as far as the 18th century liberal philosopher John Stuart Mill, who maintained:

"The capacity to see and feel what is lovable and admirable in a thing and what is laughable in it, at the same time, constitutes humor."

Because, unfortunately, obviously, this is untrue.

Instead, the sharp, dangerous, and *sardonic* side of jokes is the subject of the next chapter.

Chapter 7
Political Jokes and Cold War Humor

This World War Two recruitment poster was repurposed by the Pittsburgh Comedy Club.

Nowadays, political humor is mainstream. From the *Simpsons* to the *Onion* to all the various late-night hosts. American TV is full of jokes presented by heirs to a tradition started by Danté in his *Divine Comedy*—the one in which he depicted the politicians of his day being tortured in hell. In a moment, I'll take a close look at how jokes were one of the few forms of possible defiance for those living under the total control of governments in the Soviet Union, but first, let's look at how some more recent and contemporary politicians in the West have sought to use humor to mold public opinion.

Let's start with Ronald Reagan, a highly effective politician who disguised a sharp mind under a carefully crafted image of being just a simple guy and surely America's wittiest president. He even poked fun at his own age and reputation for laziness, saying, 'I have left orders to be awakened at any time in case of a national emergency…even if I'm in a Cabinet meeting.' Reagan was a refreshing change for countries—even other Western democracies—where jokes about an octogenarian president could lead to long prison terms.

But then, for Reagan, jokes were not just for fun but were weapons in a political armory. On October 21, 1984, in the Municipal Auditorium in Kansas City, the second debate of the presidential campaign between Reagan and former Vice President Walter Mondale provided a memorable example of the use of a joke to reset the political agenda. As part of the question-and-answer session, Henry Trewhitt of *The Baltimore Sun* brought up the fact that Reagan was the oldest president in history and compared that with the stresses of the job. Trewhitt asked President Reagan, 'Is there any doubt in your mind that you would be able to function in such circumstances?' Reagan, with a serious look that slowly developed into a smile, replied, 'Not at all, Mr. Trewhitt, and I want you to know that also I will not make age an issue of this campaign. I am not going to exploit, for political purposes, my opponent's youth and inexperience.' The audience, Mondale included, laughed heartily. Recalling the event in a 1990 interview, Mondale conceded, 'He got the audience with that, yeah. I could tell that one hurt. That was really the end of my campaign that night.'[77]

On the practical political front, America's 40th president represented a return to the interventionist economics of Franklin Roosevelt's New Deal, which involved using central government money to kickstart the economy and create jobs.

Many in his party were against such policies. Indeed, although during the 1980s, "Reaganomics" saw 20 million new jobs created, the national debt soared. So, when Reagan joked, 'The government's view of the economy could be summed up in a few short phrases: If it moves, tax it. If it keeps moving, regulate it. And if it stops moving, subsidize it,' the joke was actually doing some serious work in defanging criticisms made by his opponents.[78]

---

[77] **Chapter 7:** PBS.org September 24 2000
[78] Reagan.com April 15 2019

However, it is in Reagan's role in ending the Cold War, the most enduring crisis of the post-World War II era, that his strongest claim to success lies. And it is no coincidence that it is on this theme that he can be found telling most of his jokes, too. Here is perhaps the best example of Reagan's skillful use of jokes (which he usually referred to deprecatingly as 'his stories') to shape opinion and support policy. The cleverest part of it is that, even long after, few people realize that the jokes were political!

The important thing about Reagan was that he never *appeared* clever. By contrast, fifteen years later, Barack Obama, despite his best efforts, came across to many as a bit superior, even something of a smartarse, while his successor, Donald Trump, engaged well with "his base" but beyond it, his joking was perceived as "inappropriate", even as the behavior of a buffoon. Reagan hit the sweet spot: not stupid, not clever, just a regular guy.

Here's an example of how Reagan used humor to change the perceptions and attitudes of Americans toward Russia. (At the time when he was President, the context was decades of distrust and the Cold War.) To open the conversation, Reagan told Americans that jokes reveal Russians to have 'a great sense of humor. Also, they have a pretty cynical attitude about their government'[79] something that, of course, most of his listeners would empathize with.

According to Reagan's own account of it, given during a press conference, when his Soviet opposite number, President Gorbachev, came to Washington on a history-making state visit, to break the ice, Reagan told him a communist joke—and Gorbachev had laughed [80]. The joke, which made fun of the communist theory that a transitional era of socialism was preceding the communist utopia, went like this, 'Two men are walking down a street in Moscow. One asks the other, "Is this full communism? Have we really passed through socialism and reached full communism?" The other answers, "Hell, no. It's gonna get a lot worse first."'

It's obviously one where it's 'how you tell it.' But Reagan did have a unique, acting-polished delivery style, and whatever he said to the Russians in due course brought about a rapprochement between the United States and the Soviet Union. (Commentators have also noted how the two men's "personal chemistry" played a part).

---

[79] Reaganlibrary.gov
[80] *Prospect* May 20 2006

Another story he introduced, with a wink to the audience that this one he didn't share with Gorbachev, runs like this:

Joke #20: The New Car

There's a ten-year delay for cars in the Soviet Union for the delivery of an automobile. And only one out of seven families in the Soviet Union owns automobiles.

(All this delivered deadpan, as if given the kind of serious economic statistics that politicians normally do.)

There's a ten-year wait, and then you go through quite a process when you're ready to buy, and then you put up the money in advance and this happened to a fella, and this is their story.

This man laid down his money, and then the fella that's in charge says, 'Okay, come back in ten years and get your car,' and he's says, 'Morning or afternoon?' [*Laughter*].

And the fella behind the counter says, 'Well, ten years! What difference does it make?'

And he says, 'Well, the plumber's coming in the morning.'

[*Laughter*]

It's a great joke, and one that connects with many people's experiences of waiting for appointments or tradespeople. But through the joke, Reagan also introduces several political messages. One is that Russians are people like "us", and that they have a sense of humor. Another is that they have a political system that is less effective at getting consumer goods to people (which was surely true) and that ordinary Russians, in short, were less lucky than Americans.

Think how boring that would have been as a political message! Done as a joke though, and it is both far more enjoyable (going around people's strongly held views and prejudices rather than directly challenging them) and effective.

Reagan, sometimes dubbed 'the Great Communicator,' was an enormously popular speaker, a master of the pithy aside and the media 'sound bite.' He used his voice and sense of timing to great effect, once saying, 'I've often wondered how you could be President and not be an actor.'

What about Donald Trump, though? President Number 45 was also a kind of actor, having produced and hosted the reality TV shows *The Apprentice* and *The Celebrity Apprentice*. Trump's saving grace, and one he shared with Reagan, is that he often appears jovial, either to be telling jokes or, at the very least, to be about to tell a joke. Indeed, for arts critic Richard Zoglin, Trump looked and sounded like 'a traditional Borscht Belt comic' complete with the 'mocking rhythms, the dripping sarcasm, the exaggerated expressions, and the outlandish hyperbole.'[81] And yet, Zoglin adds, when it came to telling an actual joke, Trump was fairly hopeless.

Zoglin offers as Trump's best effort a remark, made shortly after taking office, at the Gridiron Club dinner in March 2018, when he said he would be open to a one-on-one meeting with North Korean leader Kim Jong Un. 'As for the risk of dealing with a madman is concerned,' Trump said, 'that's his problem, not mine.'[82] It's impossible to know if this was self-deprecating humor or political ineptness, though, as another feature of Trump is that he never laughed at his own jokes (or anyone else's, for that matter). One commenter on the internet put it well: 'Trump doesn't laugh. I believe he is humorless. He can be "sardonic" but that is more about mocking people than having humor.'

Nonetheless, that still leaves Trump with his sardonic side. And, according to his media handlers, he *was* often joking—only so drily that people didn't realize it. As with, for example, his appeal during the 2016 campaign to 'Russia, if you're listening,' to help find his rival Hillary Clinton's emails. This, we learned only later (in his written responses to an inquiry into Russian interference in the election), was a joke.[83] Likewise, his suggestion to police officers in 2017 'don't be too nice' when putting suspects into the backseats of squad cars was, according to the White House, another example of Trump's joshing.[84]

If so, it really must have been very dry humor. Here's part of what Trump advised the police on a visit to Long Island, New York, in July 2017.

Like when you guys put somebody in the car and you're protecting their head, you know, the way you put your hand over their head, he said, putting

[81] *Washington Post* July 5 2020
[82] HuffPost.com March 4 2018
[83] time.com April 18 2019
[84] PBS.com July 31 2017

his hand above his head for emphasis. I said, 'You can take the hand away, okay?'[85]

And then there was Trump's idea that injecting disinfectants might be a cure for the coronavirus. Just "a sarcastic question to reporters", Trump insisted after the blowback.[86]

"When I was asking a sarcastic—a very sarcastic question to the reporters in the room about disinfectant on the inside, but it does kill it, and it would kill it on the hands, and that would make things much better. That was done in the form of a sarcastic question to a reporter."

What is known is that Trump asked Dr. Deborah Birx, a scientist on the coronavirus task force, and William Bryan, head of science and technology at the Department of Homeland Security, to investigate whether light and disinfectant could be used on the human body.[87]

'So, suppose we heat the body with a tremendous, whether it's ultraviolet or just very powerful light, and I think you said that hasn't been checked, but you're going to test it,' Trump said, apparently referring to an earlier conversation.

'And then I said suppose you brought the light inside the body, which you can either do through the skin or in some other way, and I think you said you were going to test that too. Sounds interesting,' he continued before asking about an injection of a disinfectant into patients. 'And then I see the disinfectant, [which] knocks it out in a minute. One minute. And is there a way we can do something like that, by injection inside or almost a cleaning…It'll be interesting to check that,' the president said.

All of which underline the importance of context. If it's presidents holding a meeting with their experts to look at possible strategies in a medical crisis, that's obviously not the kind of context to sardonically suggest absurd solutions.

Jokes are useful to politicians for camouflage and allow them to float controversial ideas that otherwise could be politically dangerous. The journalist and TV critic Emily Nussbaum worries that for politicians, a joke can be another kind of Big Lie, 'shrunk to look like a toy.' It's the thrill of hyperbole, of treating the extreme as normal, and the shock (and the joy) of

---

[85] HuffPost.com July 28 2017

[86] *New York Post* 24 April 2020

[87] *New York Post* 24 April 2020

seeing the normal get violated fast. She says, 'The Big Lie is a propaganda technique: state false facts so outlandish that they must be true, because who would make up something so crazy?'[88] The accusation could fit many politicians, but indeed, Nussbaum had in mind a particular target, the populist and larger-than-life figure of Donald Trump.

'Buh-leeve me, buh-leeve me!' Trump said it in his act, again and again. Lying about telling the truth is part of the joke. Saying 'This really happened!' creates trust, even if what the audience trusts you to do is to keep on tricking them, like a magician reassuring you that while his other jokes are tricks, this one is magic.

Ms. Nussbaum distinguishes between two kinds of political jokers: the hot ones and the cool ones. Trump is a hot comic; Obama was a cool one. As for Hillary Clinton, Trump's defeated opponent for the Presidency, she 'had the skill to be hard-funny too, when it was called for: she killed at the Al Smith charity dinner in New York, while Trump bombed. It didn't matter, though, because that was not the role she fitted the popular imagination in.'

This was because, Nussbaum surmises, she was a woman. Women struggle to be accepted as comics—a point I'll return to in another chapter. 'Trump might be thin-skinned and easily offended, a grafter C.E.O. on a literal golden throne. But Hillary matched the look and the feel of Margaret Dumont: the rich bitch, Nurse Ratched, the buzzkill, the no-fun mom...'

I'm afraid that Hillary really did come across like that. But it's not maybe just because she was a woman. After all, there are plenty of successful woman comics—and even 'no-fun mom'; Margaret Thatcher frequently had audiences laughing at her jokes.

The British politician who really has a reputation as something of a joker, though, is Boris Johnson, who was Mayor of London for many years before becoming the British Foreign Secretary in 2016 and Prime Minister five years later.

Many years prior to actually being responsible himself for implementing policies, Johnson had made a name for himself as a journalist, dashing off humorous articles in British newspapers alleging outlandish things of his favored political bogeyman, the remote-seeming and bureaucratic European Union, such as that it was attempting to impose standard condom sizes on UK

---

[88] *The New Yorker,* January 23 2017

males or to ban bendy bananas—stories all cheerfully indifferent to the facts. When he was actually in power, he carried on in the same style, making similarly factually incorrect claims, such as about how much money the UK paid the European Union every week, or whether Turkey was really about to join the EU, as part of a national referendum campaign, to the extent that it was never clear whether he believed what he was saying and was wrong, or was being witty and cocking his snoot at stuffy notions of public discourse and truthfulness.

Thus, for example, in 2017, while he was in the role of chief British diplomat, or Foreign Secretary, Boris Johnson, quipped that Libya, recovering from a bloody civil war, could become 'a new Dubai' but only if it cleared the dead bodies away. The actual words he used are more offensive than the summaries offered in news reports:

'They've got a brilliant vision to turn Sirte, with the help of the municipality of Sirte, into the next Dubai,' Johnson said. 'The only thing they've got to do is clear the dead bodies away, and then we will be there.' *Reuters* reported[89] that activists from Prime Minister Theresa May's party laughed uproariously at this before the chair of the event changed the subject, saying, 'Next question.'

But for the wider British public, the joke hit a duff note. Uncharacteristically backtracking, Johnson explained in a series of late-night posts on Twitter that he had been referring seriously to the clearing of booby-trapped bodies of Islamic State militant fighters. It's likely his civil servants had proposed the new line.

All of which reminds me of a joke featuring President George W. Bush (the younger one) and his Secretary of Defense, Donald Rumsfeld.

Joke #21: Big Numbers

Rumsfeld is giving the president his daily briefing. He concludes it by saying, 'Yesterday, three Brazilian soldiers were killed.' At this, President Bush unexpectedly exclaims, 'OH NO! That's terrible!'

His staff are surprised at this display of emotion and watch nervously as the President sits, shuddering, head in hands.

---

[89] Reuters October 4 2017

Finally, the President looks up and asks, 'Uh, how many exactly is a *brazillion*?'

There were a lot of jokes about the younger Bush presidency, and indeed, they may have nibbled away at his credibility until, despite having started out with approval ratings at record highs, he left office as one of the least popular presidents ever. Something similar seems to have happened to Boris Johnson in Britain. No longer able to waft away criticism with a chuckle, he started to labor under the perception of being not only a lightweight but a liar and a fraud. The joke, so to speak, ended up being on him.

Which brings me to a more general observation about jokes. And this is that, as Freud says, the discovery that it is in our control to make another person comical is itself a form of political power. And that this is really the case and not just a nice idea, was brought out by a high-profile study called 'The Project on the Soviet Social Systems' that was commissioned at Harvard University in the 1950s by the US government (and the CIA) as part of an openly anti-Soviet agenda[90]. Years after that original CIA exercise in gathering evidence of anti-Soviet humor, Ronald Reagan ordered the State Department to collect the fruits and send them to him in weekly memos. Paul Goble, head of the Balkans desk in the 1980s, assembled a collection of 15,000 communist jokes (although I suspect most of them were basically the same with different details).

Anyway, back in the nineteen fifties, over a period of two years, the Harvard sociologists interviewed around 600 Russian refugees located in camps in Western Europe. They soon discovered that when asked to describe their lives in Russia, the refugees often told jokes. One of the most popular (perhaps because they directly spoke to their own situation) was the so-called Orphan joke. This runs:

Joke #22: Family Fortunes

A teacher asks a pupil: Who is your mother and who is your father?

The pupil replies, My mother is Russian, and my father is Stalin.

'Very good!' says the teacher. 'And now, what would you like to be when you grow up?'

'An orphan.'

---

[90] harvard.edu

Commenting on the remark in 1956, the *New York Times Magazine* wrote: 'A bitter humor with a strong sense of irony but no pity…has served to keep up the spirits of the people during…Communist rule.'[91]

Another joke retold by Dan Hill, the author of various books, all broadly on how to understand people, an approach that he calls "Emotionomics", concerns what he calls the 'essential dourness to Eastern Europe'[92]. It runs.

Joke #23: You Get Just One Wish

A man receives a visit from his fairy godmother, and she says he can have whatever he wishes for. But of course, there's a catch, which is that whatever it is that he wishes for…will be given to his worst enemy two-fold—twice as good! So, if he wishes for a new car, his worst enemy will have two lovely new cars.

So, what does the man request? Why is *that one of his eyes gouged out?*

As I say, Dan Hill is trying to understand people and predict their responses—both serious matters and useful skills, as well as part of the broader philosophical quest. What, for example, do such jokes tell us about people like Vladimir Putin, the heroic leader of the Great Russian nation to his fans but the butcher of Chechnya and the hypocritical warmonger of Ukraine for many others? Indeed, history seems to show that the ex-KGB man would seem exactly the sort to make such a crafty and horrid wish.

The joke does give a psychological insight into the thinking of many Eastern European cultures and certainly provides a different framework for understanding people's reactions. It suggests that Russians will not be dissuaded from wars by (for example) crippling economic sanctions or even losing the right to host the football World Cup!—as long as they feel sure that *harm* is being done to their rivals.

The joke also reminds me of the bitter dispute between the Greeks and the Germans over their debts to the European Bank, which threatened their continued membership of the Euro currency zone. Part of the problem with these negotiations has been that it is Western Europe talking to Eastern

---

[91] Quoted at BenLewisProjects.com 22 July, 2007
[92] JapanTimes.co.jp June 11 2015

Europe—Mars to Venus! Greece is actually part of the economic world of the European Union, but culturally and socially, it has more affinity with Russia.

Dimitris Stratoulis, the Greek Social Security Minister, put the "eye-gouging out" policy very bluntly in an interview just before what was heralded as the last chance meeting for Greeks to stay in the Euro: If we are forced to say "the big no", the difficulties will last for us for a few months…but the consequences *will be much worse for Europe.*

But back to Eastern Europe and the years of the Cold War. And always, the idea that the jokes were a form of resistance to Communism was, in the words of Ben Lewis (author of a book of political jokes, *Hammer and Tickle: A History of Communism Told Through Communist Jokes)* 'overlaid on the facts' with the enthusiastic support of the disaffected Soviet émigrés. It was argued on their behalf that jokes could restate a people's cultural identity and remind them of who they really were.

Throughout the 1950s, the *New York Times Magazine* would devote pages to jokes drawn from the Harvard project. And, from the 1960s onwards, volumes of communist jokes were published in paperback form in Europe and North America. But most influential of all, the *New York Times* itself, a paper that then (and for all I know still does) had a senior journalist seconded from the CIA on it[93], started to run regular features describing the "underground" culture of Russian jokes.

It seemed that there was truth in George Orwell's notion of every joke as 'a tiny revolution.' This is how that British writer, author of, among other things, *Animal Farm,* itself a searing parody of life in the Soviet Union, put it in a little known 1945 essay called 'Funny, but not Vulgar'[94]:

"A thing is funny when, in some way that is not actually offensive or frightening, it upsets the established order. Every joke is a tiny revolution. If you had to define humor in a single phrase, you might define it as dignity sitting on a tintack. Whatever destroys dignity and brings down the mighty from their seats, preferably with a bump, is funny. The bigger they fall, the bigger the joke. It would be better fun to throw a custard pie at a bishop than at a curate."

However, as Orwell himself went on to add, humor is not *really* as politically subversive as it pretends. A joke is a temporary rebellion against

---

[93] NYT.com December 1 1973
[94] Orwell.ru

virtue, and its aim is not to degrade the human being but to remind him that it is already degraded. A willingness to make extremely obscene jokes can coexist with very strict moral standards, as in pillars of literature like Chaucer, Shakespeare, and Dickens.

Nonetheless, in the Soviet Union, the monopoly of state power meant that any act of non-conformity, even the tiniest one, could be construed as a form of dissent, and a joke about anything could be interpreted as a critique of Communism. Which explains why, when the historian Roy Medvedev looked through the files of Stalin's political prisoners, he concluded that hundreds of thousands of people were imprisoned for telling jokes[95]. Ones like this:

Joke #24: The Prisoners

Three prisoners in the gulag get to talking about why they are there. 'I am here because I always got to work five minutes late, and they charged me with sabotage,' says the first prisoner. 'I am here because I kept getting to work five minutes early, and they charged me with spying,' says the second. At this, the third one pipes up. 'I am here because I got to work on time every day!' The others are intrigued by this, so he explains further: 'They charged me with owning a Western watch!'

Many jokes capture the schizophrenic nature of the clampdown on subversive humor.

Joke #25: The Naughty Parrot

A frightened man came to the KGB. 'My talking parrot has disappeared.' 'That's not the kind of case we handle. Go to the criminal police.' 'Excuse me; of course I know that I must go to them. I am here just to tell you officially that I disagree with the parrot.'

Or consider this one in which a judge walks out of his chambers, chuckling cheerfully to himself. A colleague approaches him and asks why he is laughing. 'I just heard a wonderful joke!' 'Well, go ahead, tell me!' says the second judge. 'I can't—I just gave a guy ten years for it!'

Often, Cold War humor seems to take pleasure in referring back on itself. Another joke that (potentially at least) does this is this one[96]:

---

[95] Lewis 2011, 7

[96] en.wikipedia.org Russian Jokes

Q: Will there be any need for a state secret police under Communism?

A: As you know, in Communism, the state will be abolished, together with its means of suppression. People will know how to self-arrest themselves.

To fully appreciate this joke, the listener needs to know a little about the ideology of Communism. The original version was about the Cheka, Russia's first secret police, during which time, peasants were often forced to perform *samooblozhenie* (self-taxation), and prosperous peasants, especially *kulaks*, were expected to "voluntarily" deliver the same amount of agricultural products again, with the amounts being set at collective meetings.

The schizophrenia of life in the Soviet Union also led to jokes about the police spying on people and telling jokes, like this one.

Joke #26: The Interruption

Scene: a hotel in Moscow and a shared room with four strangers. Three of them soon open a bottle of vodka at the table and proceed to get acquainted, then drunk, then become noisy, singing and telling political jokes. The fourth one lies in his bunk bed and desperately tries to get some sleep. Finally, frustrated, he leaves the room, goes downstairs, and asks the concierge to bring tea to Room 67 in ten minutes.

Then he returns, and this time he joins in the game of cards. Five minutes later, he bends over an ashtray and says in an everyday voice, 'Uh, Comrade, some tea to Room 67, please.' His bemused companions pause for a moment at this, but then carry on playing as before. However, in a few minutes, there's a knock at the door, and in comes the lady concierge with a tea tray. The room falls silent, and the party stops. In this way, the conspirator finally gets to sleep. The next morning, he wakes up alone in the room.

Surprised, he runs downstairs and asks the concierge where his roommates have gone. 'Oh, the KGB has arrested them!' she answers. 'B-but…but what about me?' asks the guy in horror. 'Oh, well, they decided to let you go. The Colonel liked your tea gag a lot.'

Other jokes regularly mutate to fit changing news and circumstances. This one has had many different protagonists, most of whom have now vanished into the mists of history, so I have slightly updated it for the 21st century with a nod at the revelations of so-called enhanced interrogation techniques in the notorious, secret CIA-run prisons.

Joke #27: Cruelty to Rabbits

The British Secret Service, the KGB, and the CIA are all trying to prove that they are the best at catching criminals. The Secretary General of the UN decides to give them a test. He releases a rabbit into a forest, and each of them has to catch it. The British go in first. They place animal informants throughout the forest. They questioned all plant and mineral witnesses. After three months of extensive investigations, they conclude that the rabbit does not exist.

The KGB goes in next. After two weeks with no leads, they burn the forest, killing everything in it, including the rabbit, and make no apologies: the rabbit had it coming.

The CIA went in last. They came out two hours later with a badly disturbed bear, foaming at the mouth. The bear is yelling, 'Okay! Okay! I'm a rabbit! I'm a rabbit!'

According to Ben Lewis, in that *Prospect Magazine* article[97], following the fall of the Hungarian regime, the archives of the secret police were discovered to be full of dossiers concerning people arrested for telling jokes. 'Day in, day out, officers of the state were taking the time and trouble to track down joke-tellers, or going out of their way to add the evidence of joke-telling to other charges, and then handing out short sentences.'

As Lewis says, 'Communist jokes were a way to criticize and outmaneuver the system, but they were also something more than this. They comprised a secret language between citizens—membership of a club to which the government was not invited...'

Many governments have passed special laws limiting political jokes, including Western democracies like France, but few went as far as the Soviet Union, where the term *Anekdot* is the special Russian word for a political joke and where "anti-Soviet propaganda" was a potentially capital offense.

However, most jokes there relate to everyday life, in particular the inefficiencies and economic failings of Soviet rule, rather than directly attacking the system itself.

Joke #28: Capitalist Hell

A man dies and goes to hell. There he discovers that he has a choice: he can go to Capitalist Hell or to Communist Hell. Naturally, he wants to compare

---

[97] *Prospect* May 20 2006

the two, so he goes over to Capitalist Hell. There, outside the door, is a devil. 'What's it like in there?' asks the visitor. 'Well,' the devil replies coldly, 'in Capitalist Hell, they flay you alive, then they boil you in oil, and then they cut you up into small pieces with sharp knives.'

'That's terrible!' he gasps. 'I'm going to check out Communist Hell!' He goes over to where it is, but discovers a huge queue of people waiting to get in. He waits in line. Eventually he gets to the front, and there at the door is another little devil. 'Please, devil, I've still got the choice of Capitalist Hell to enter, so before I come in, I want to know what it's like in there.'

'In Communist Hell,' says the devil impatiently, 'they flay you alive, then they boil you in oil, and then they cut you up into small pieces with sharp knives.'

'But...but that's the same as Capitalist Hell!' protests the man, 'Why such a long queue?'

'Well,' sighs the devil, 'Sometimes we're out of oil, sometimes we don't have knives, sometimes no hot water...'

At times, apart from arresting and "re-educating" people in camps, the Soviets tried to make joking itself socially unacceptable. Ben Lewis recalls (Prospect, May 20, 2006) that there were letters railing against the flood of jokes, like this one from *Izvestia* in 1964.

Dear Sir,

Ten days ago, I went to our savings bank. In front of the clerk's window, there were five people waiting for their turn. And while standing there, I heard too much. There were two of them in front of me, well fed, healthy, and really well dressed...and in a public place, with an insolent casualness, they were trying to outdo each other, swapping their "best" political jokes. How can I restrain myself in front of these "jokers", who tell me mockingly a 'new anecdote?' Nothing is sacred to them. They spit on everything! We have to fight them; it is necessary to discredit, shame, and dishonor them in front of honest people.

With deep respect, Nikolay Kuritsin
External student, Kadykchan village.

Don't wait for the punchline, because there isn't one!

However, the extent to which such campaigns failed to re-educate Soviet citizens away from their dry, satirical, and self-critical sense of humor is shown by the fact that when President Gorbachev, Russia's most important reforming leader, visited the United Kingdom following the collapse of the Berlin Wall and the liberation of most of Eastern Europe, the first thing he did when he appeared on the Clive Anderson talk show in Britain was himself to offer a subversive *anekdot*, featuring himself in the leader's role.

Joke #29: The Longest Queue

A Soviet man is waiting in line to purchase vodka from a liquor store. However, due to restrictions imposed by the government, the line is excessively long. The man loses his nerve and screams, 'I can't take this waiting in line anymore. I HATE the president. I am going to the Kremlin right now, and I am going to kill him!' After 40 minutes, the man returns and begins elbowing his way back to the vodka in place. They begin to ask if he succeeded in killing the president, to which the man replies: 'No, I got to the Kremlin, but the line to kill him was far too long, so I decided to come back and wait for my vodka.'

Gorbachev was far from the only Russian president to enjoy the odd joke. More ominously, Stalin himself cracked them too, including this one about a visit from a Georgian delegation[98]. In the *anekdot*, the delegates come, they talk to Stalin, and then they go, heading off down the Kremlin's corridors. Stalin starts looking for his pipe. He can't find it. He calls in Beria, the head of his secret police. 'Go after the delegation and find out which one took my pipe,' he says. Beria scuttles off down the corridor. Five minutes later, Stalin finds his pipe under a pile of papers. He calls Beria—Look, I've found my pipe.' 'It's too late,' Beria says, 'half the delegation admitted they took your pipe, and the other half died during questioning.'

That French philosopher of humor, Henri Bergson again, thinks that if someone detects a defect in their behavior to the extent that they can start to laugh at it, then the defect is on the way to being remedied, but Stalin's laughter instead underlines the deeper cynicism of the Soviet enterprise and many

---

[98] cato.org

cruelties since. At least, it can perhaps be allowed that the joke is not actually "racist", as Stalin himself was Georgian by birth.

Here's another Stalin joke. It starts with the Father of the Nation reading the Soviet Annual Report to the Party Congress. Suddenly, someone sneezes. 'Who sneezed?' shouts Stalin. (*Silence.*) 'First row! On your feet! Shoot them!' (*Applause.*) 'Who sneezed?' (*Silence.*) 'Second row! On your feet! Shoot them!' (Applause.) 'Who sneezed?' (*Silence.*) A dejected voice in the back: 'It was me' (*Sobs.*) Stalin leans forward and points a finger at the terrified man. 'Bless you, comrade!'

I think it is a fine joke, but it rests unambiguously on a very sinister characterization of Stalin.

This next joke relies on a shared assessment of President Brezhnev, who led the Soviet Union from 1964 to 1982, and that he was in poor health, verging on senility, for much of the latter period. After the speech, Brezhnev confronts his speechwriter. 'I asked for a 15-minute speech, but the one you gave me lasted 45 minutes!' The speechwriter replies, 'I gave you three copies…'

If the collapse of the Berlin Wall and the liberalization of Russia and Eastern Europe made political jokes less interesting, just as they were allowed, it seems that under Vladimir Putin, political jokes regained popularity. And if the Cold War officially ended a long time ago, in a world of jokes, stereotypes hang on, and so many play on Putin's KGB background, such as this one in which Stalin's ghost appears to Putin in a dream. Of course, Putin asks for his help running the country. Stalin says, 'Round up and shoot all the democrats, and then paint the inside of the Kremlin blue.' 'Why blue?' Putin asks. 'Ha!' says Stalin. 'I knew you wouldn't ask me about the first part.'

In another, a man is reported to have said, 'Putin is a moron!' and is arrested by a Russian policeman. 'No, sir, I meant not our respected leader, but another `Putin!' he protests. 'Don't try to trick me' snaps back the policeman, 'If you say "moron," you are obviously referring to our president!'

Russians like jokes that play with the "referents" of words, as philosophers might say. Another slightly more sophisticated version runs like this.

Joke #30: Stalin's Mustachio

During the Second World War, a secretary is standing outside the Kremlin as Marshal Zhukov, the most important Russian general in World War Two, leaves a meeting with Stalin, and she hears him muttering under his breath,

'Mustachioed idiot!' She immediately rushes in to see Stalin and breathlessly reports, 'I just heard Zhukov say, "Mustachioed idiot"!'

Stalin dismisses the secretary and sends for Zhukov, who comes back in. 'And just who did you have in mind with this talk of "mustachioed idiots"?' asks Stalin. 'Why, Adolf Hitler, of course!' replies Zhukov, trembling.

Apparently satisfied, Stalin thanks him, dismisses him, and then calls the secretary back and explains what the Marshal had said. 'And now, who did you think he was talking about?'

You have to laugh at this joke, with its deeply sinister undertones. And in addition, there is an element of "just desserts" in the informer-secretary's predicament.

But back to "real life" and when Vladimir Putin was elected president, in 2000, one of his first acts was to kill "Kukly", a sketch puppet show that portrayed him as Little Tsaches, a sinister baby who uses a "magic TV comb" to bewitch a city—a humorous reworking of a German folktale in which a fairy casts a spell on an ugly dwarf so that others find him irresistibly beautiful. Putin's predecessor, Mr. Yeltsin, put up for years with the satirical barbs of the TV puppet and even intervened when officials talked of prosecuting the makers of the show, NTV. But media management meant something rather different to Mr. Yeltsin's KGB-trained protégé. Putin simply threatened to shut down the channel unless it removed the puppet. NTV refused. Within months, it was under state control. According to *Newsweek*, 'Putin jokes quickly vanished from Russia's television screens.'

President Putin himself doesn't "do" jokes, at least not in the funny sense. He once remarked to a child, 'Russia's borders don't end anywhere'—before adding, 'That's a joke.'[99]

Perhaps President Putin would have allowed this joke, though. It starts with the scene of two friends walking down a street.

One asks the other, 'What do you think of the president?'

'I can't tell you here,' he replies.

'Follow me.' They disappear down a side street.

'Now, tell me what you think of the president,' says the friend.

---

[99] news.com.au

'No, not here,' says the other, leading him into the hallway of an apartment block.

'OK, here then.'

'No, not here. It's not safe.' They walk down the stairs into the deserted basement of the building.

'OK, now you can tell me what you think of our president.'

'Well,' says the other, looking around nervously, 'actually I quite admire him.'[100]

The idea of "good" political jokes was central to a satirical magazine called *Eulenspiegel,* which appeared in communist East Germany in the years before the building of the Berlin Wall and the Cold War proper. The title was a reference to both a fictional prankster in German folklore and also suggested 'wise humor,' and the magazine was supposed to be the communist state's official organ of humor. There were to be no limits on its jokes, no censorship, as the East Germans were so proud of telling the readers. Instead, freed from overt state interference, the editors instead had the more difficult task of intuiting which gags were politically acceptable. As a result, every week the magazine carried pages of childish and politically neutral slapstick, but there was also "politically correct" humor, in which capitalists in top hats counted their money and American soldiers enslaved Africans. Some pages of the magazine can be found on the internet, which reveal its basically trivial nature.

Eulenspiegel once tried to make common cause with *Pardon*, its West German left-wing counterpart. After all, *Pardon* also attacked Adenauer and American imperialism. But the editors of *Eulenspiegel* were stung when *Pardon* rebuffed their advances, on the grounds that the communist satirists failed to criticize their own leader, Walter Ulbricht, also known as 'The Father of the Berlin Wall.'

The editors of *Euelenspiegel* printed a response entitled 'How do we write about Walter Ulbricht?' in 1963, patiently (humorously) explaining:

"The transparency and virtue of our state make it not only difficult but simply impossible to write a satire about its representatives. Where there is nothing to uncover, the satirist will find no material. So how do we satirists write about Walter Ulbricht? We send our greetings and best wishes to the first

---

[100] *Prospect* May 20 2006

secretary of the central committee. We wish Comrade Ulbricht health, stamina, and a long life."

(Reprinted in *Prospect,* May 20, 2006)

It's funny…in a sense, I suppose.

The spat between the two Germany's raises an old debate about that nation's sense of humor. While Russians are proud of their jokes tradition, which seems to be a sort of social response, a safety valve, for a grossly unequal and harsh society, joke experts have been puzzled as to why, by comparison, Germany under the Nazis left so few evidence of the existence of an underground, resistance humor—even if there was however a lively tradition of jokes within the Jewish community such as 'What is the difference between a Jewish optimist and a Jewish pessimist? The pessimist is in exile, and the optimist is in a concentration camp.'[101]

For the joke analyst Ben Lewis, at least, it seems that the reason that within Germany there were very few jokes about Hitler, either about his racist ideology or the Nazi's bizarre rituals, is something to do with the German sense of humor, or to be precise, a deficiency with it. Lewis says he found no contemporary jokes mentioning even relatively anodyne things like Hitler's mustache or the Nazi soldiers' goose-stepping.

On the other hand, he found reports that one comedian. Weiss Ferdl actually did warm-up routines for Hitler, repeated for Hitler, and told this joke about a visit he had made to the already notorious concentration camp of Dachau: 'It looked amazing: barbed wire, machine guns, and over there more machine guns and more barbed wire. But I'll tell you one thing: if I want to get into the place, I'll find a way somehow!'[102]

If the gag might seem to have been dryly ironic, the fact remains that Weiss Ferdl, was a member of the Nazi Party and was convicted of collaboration after the war. Of course, the fact that Lewis did not find many jokes about the Nazis does not mean that they weren't told. Only that, under the brutal efficiency of the Nazi regime, they had to be kept very firmly "underground" and few traces survived.

After all, there are some anti-Nazi memes that we do know circulate. One slight witticism, Lewis also recalls, concerned Hitler's right-hand man, Air Marshal Goering. After the Reichstag, the German parliament, was set on fire

---

[101] Hillenbrand FKM, 7

[102] Lewis 2011, 30

by the Nazis in 1933, this joke circulated. It runs: On the evening of February 27, Goering's adjutant rushed into the office of his superior. 'Herr, MisterPraesident,' he says. 'Something terrible has happened! The Reichstag is on fire!' Goering looks at his watch and shakes his head in amazement: 'Already!'

Another one in the same spirit, also noted by Lewis, goes like this:

"Goering's adjutant rushed into the office of his superior. 'Herr, MisterPraesident,' he says. 'There's an emergency: a pipe has burst in the offices of the Air Ministry and is threatening to flood the whole building!' Goering leaps to his feet and says, 'Quick, bring me my admiral's uniform!'"

But such levity was before 1939, the year war was declared in Europe and the year Goebbels wrote in his diary: 'We will eradicate the political joke'[103]. And after this, there are cases of people being executed solely for telling them, such as the film actor Robert Dorsay, who was executed in 1943 on the orders of Judge Freisler, who ran a court dedicated to dealing with 'political crimes.'

Among the jokes attributed to Dorsay was this one:

One day, the Führer visits town and is greeted by girls holding bouquets of flowers that they have picked. One of the girls, however, offers a bouquet consisting of long grasses. 'What shall I do with this?' asks the Führer benevolently. 'Eat it, please,' says the girl. 'People are saying that the good times will only return when you eat grass.'

It's not even a very funny joke.

However, efforts to ban political jokes are never likely to succeed. After all, politicians themselves like them too much.

Two thousand years ago, Cicero, the Ancient Roman philosopher and statesman, noted that jokes fit naturally into political speeches because they are powerful oratorical devices. In what is probably the most extensive ancient treatment of humor, *De Oratore,* Cicero's appropriately named guide to the skills of oratory, warns that being funny is not so easy and that all those "who have attempted to deliver rules and principles on that subject, have shown themselves so extremely foolish, that nothing else in them has excited laughter but their folly."[104]

---

[103] Jelavich, Peter 2021, chapter 8
[104] Cicero, 2.217

Cicero's cold thought is that it is in the orator's interest to make the audience laugh to secure goodwill, demonstrate cleverness, or attack an opponent. It is in this practical quest that he goes on to identify two types of witticisms: those of content and those of words. Witticisms of content are anecdotes or funny stories, whereas witticisms of words are to be found in puns and "sharp-witted" comments. As to the subjects appropriate for humor, Cicero places no limit on them, saying: 'Not to be tedious, there is no subject for jest from which serious and grave reflections may not be drawn'[105]. Perhaps with his eye on his relations with the emperor, however, Cicero adds that orators should avoid joking about people held in very high or very low esteem. The same caution surely applies even to stand-up comics today.

Cicero chooses as the ideal political tactic the exploitation of *humorous incongruity*. This, after eliminating clownish behavior, imitation, distortion of the face, and obscenity, Thousands of years later, it seems that the better stand-up comedians reach similar conclusions. For Cicero, the key factor is that most jokes create an expectation, and that humor is generated when the expectation is not realized. "The most common kind of joke is that in which we expect one thing, and another is said; here our own disappointed expectation makes us laugh."

"Disappointed expectations" are clearly something politicians are the experts in, yet here clearly is a strand of wit that they should be wary of!

_____

[105] Cicero, 2.250

Chapter 8
Paradoxical Jokes

The American philosopher Charles Sanders Peirce was fascinated by philosophical paradoxes, and if he didn't really solve any, he surely put his finger on something with his theory that discovery, knowledge, and experience all start with the 'pedagogy of surprise.'

Puzzle #5: The Elusive Mistake

This joke has four mistakes in it. true or false?

Well, the three mistakes are easy enough: "mistakes" has been spelled incorrectly, "for" and "four" have been confused, and "true" needed a capital letter. It is the fourth mistake that is more elusive and paradoxical. The number of errors in the joke is only three, not four. On the other hand, this error itself surely counts as an error, so there are four errors in the joke! But then, if there are indeed four errors, this final one, the-error-of-not-getting-the-number-of-errors-right disappears.

Many jokes contain paradoxes, which, despite being just silly in everyday terms, conceal considerable philosophical complexity. Kant gives as an example of a paradoxical joke the problem of paying mourners to look sadder—the problem being that the more that they are paid, the less sad they feel! But this particular one is a variation on the old philosophical paradox known as the Liar, which at its most simple runs: *Everything I say is untrue.* If the speaker is telling the truth, then not everything they say is untrue after all, at least on this occasion. So, they are lying, which fits their claim, but then, if they are lying, this one sentence is true, which contradicts their claim!

Perhaps the most persuasive example is the two-sentence paradox, which runs:

The claim made in the sentence below is false.

The claim made in the sentence above is true.

Try it and see! It is this kind of head-whirling thing that riddles appeal to.

The following puzzle—or is it a riddle? Whichever term seems better to you, seems on the face of it to ban an exercise in applied logic. If x then y, et cetera. Of course, plenty of philosophers take it that way. But lurking within it, as I'll explain after you've had a chance to puzzle over it, is something much more fuzzy, much more psychological—even paradoxical—and more interesting.

The puzzle concerns something, rather grandly, called 'Logical Time.' This was the subject of a 1945 essay by the French psychoanalyst, Jacques Lacan.[106] To be sure, he did not invent the riddle, which has ancient roots, but his version created a huge amount of new interest in it. The puzzle is a subtle exploration of how what we, as individuals, know depends intimately on what other people around us seem to know.

Here is my own, gently revised version of Lacan's philosophical teaser.

---

[106] **Chapter 8**. Baily et al 2018, 141

Puzzle #6: The Puzzle of Logical Time

The warden of a prison finds he has too many prisoners and decides to release one through a little competition. To start with, he summons three of his most favored prisoners, favored because he thinks they are very rational and logical kinds of people, and makes the following surprise announcement:

'Today, I must free one of you. In order to decide which, I have devised a test that will also evaluate your ability to reason logically.'

'Here, on my desk, I have five colored disks: three white and two black. In a moment, I will fix one disk for each of you in such a way that no prisoner can directly see their own disk but can only see those of their companions. You will all be left in a room and allowed to observe each other, but not to communicate. In any case, it would not be in anyone's interest to offer any information, as only the first person to correctly deduce the color of the disk on their back will be freed.'

'Oh, one more thing. To reduce the temptation to guess the color of your disk, I will add the small extra provision that you must properly explain your reasoning—and that in any case, a wrong guess will result in an additional punishment.'

'Now, as soon as one of you is ready to state the color of the disk on their back, you should pass through this door so that you may be judged individually on the basis of your response.'

After this, the three prisoners carefully examine each other's backs in silence. There has been a pause for some time the "logical time" during which no one moves but each regards the other. And then one of them makes a sudden dash for the door. He's allowed through and blurts out triumphantly the color of the disk on his back!

'It's white!'

Don't worry if you can't work this one out; after all, unlike the prisoners, you've got a pretty good chance of getting it right just by guessing. But in fact, the answer is concealed in the tale, and the disk is white. So how did our smart prisoners know?

The starting point is the observation that evidently, after inspecting the disks on each other's backs, none of them have enough information to simply deduce the color of the disk on their own back. On the face of it, this is bad news.

Yet, in fact, further information is available to each if they take into account the reactions of the others. In particular, because there were only two black disks, evidently none of the prisoners observed two black disks on their companions' backs, because if they did so, then they would immediately have known their own disk was white and would have run to the door. Ah-ha! Or if not "ah-ha", certainly "ahem". It's not so difficult to work out.

But now what if, instead, the warder attached one black disk to one prisoner and two whites to the others? Well, then one prisoner will find two white disks, and two prisoners will find one white and one black disk.

Now here is the trick: The real "ah-ha" moment! If a prisoner observes that one of their companions has a white disk and the other a black disk, they will know that the disk on their back is white! Because otherwise, as mentioned above, that prisoner with the white disk would have come across "two black disks" and known that the one on their own back was white. The *absence* of anyone immediately dashing to the door gives the warden's game away.

So, the warden cannot have attached a black disk to any of the prisoners' backs. Thus, any logically minded prisoner will eventually realize that the disk on their back must be white.

In real life, of course, there could be some room for doubt. How long does a pause count as "evidence" that none of the prisoners sees two black disks? A mischievous prisoner (after all, these people must be in prison for some reason) might be waiting simply in order to confuse his companions…

Philosophers have spilled much ink on the problem saying, among other things, that it sheds light on knowledge of "the Other" and on the way that each of us can only establish our identity through 'the Other's gaze.' You discover what you are by observing the reactions of those around you, and even more subtly, you become what you are because everyone around you sees you that way! Comics know this very well, as for them, the audience is 'the Other.'

Yet, at root, the problem is not at all metaphysical, merely logical. The knowledge of the color of the three disks is clearly shared among the participants, with communication reduced to observation of each other's actions. Nonetheless, there remains a paradoxical element.

This means that each prisoner's knowledge of the answer depends on the other prisoners' ignorance. It is only by observing what his fellow prisoners 'do not know' that each can draw the extra conclusion. Even more paradoxical is that any prisoner could make the inference, and once they have done so, they are no longer ignorant. In being able to deduce the color, they in a sense undermine the reasoning that allows for the deduction in the first place.

To be honest, this joke is so complicated that it gives me a bit of a headache. But what I find intriguing about it is the element of "logical time". The idea that knowledge is not entirely in your own experience but is shared collectively.

Here's a problem, one of a genre called "situation puzzles" to give your brain a rest, that is much simpler.

Puzzle #7: The Man Who Got Stressed out by a Piece of Paper

A man walks up to a tree, tears off a piece of paper pinned there, scrumples it up in a ball, throws it to the ground, and starts weeping.

A little later, he gets up, re-pins the piece of paper, and walks off again, but returns early the next day. Again, he tears off the piece of paper pinned there, scrumples it up, and starts weeping again.

Why?

This is a situation puzzle, also called a lateral thinking puzzle. In these puzzles, the task is to offer an explanation that fits the facts—the situation. There could be many answers, which is democratic, and, of course, some are funnier than others. One rather sad explanation a friend offered me was that the man had lost his dog and had put a notice appealing for information on the tree, but there never was any. That works! Not very funny, though.

The official answer to this one is very simple: The man has been wandering lost in a forest. His behavior is explained by his fear, he has been walking in circles. We can hypothesize that to test this, he pins a piece of paper to a tree. Maybe he writes a message too, such as, 'If anyone finds this, I am heading north,' but such details are not really necessary. All that matters is that he pins the piece of paper to the tree and sets off again. When, much later and exhausted, he encounters the paper again, his fears are confirmed, and fearing that he will never find his way out, he starts to weep. And as with Lacan's grander puzzle, the element of time is a vital part of the story.

Here's another puzzle in which time again plays a role. It originated in a speech given by one Don Harper Mills, at the time president of the American

Academy of Forensic Sciences, and so, yes, there is an element of the "in-joke" to all this, as the Academy's annual dinner. Curiously, the story was picked up and began to circulate on the internet, at which point, as with many internet stories, the origin and context were lost, and it assumed the status of an urban legend.

Puzzle #8: The Ambiguous Death of Ronald Opus

Ronald Opus was a young New York man who, one day, apparently very depressed, threw himself off the top of the apartment block that he lived in.

Afterwards, a postmortem was conducted, and it found that he had not died from the fall but from a gunshot injury that he had sustained while passing a window on the way down. Because of the fleeting moment he would have passed the window, there is no suggestion that the shot could have been deliberately aimed.

The examiner was unsure how to classify the death. Normally, if a person intends to commit suicide and his actions lead directly to his death, it is suicide, even if the death does not take place in quite the way the person expected.

Given all this information, how would you classify death? Homicide or suicide?

It then turns out, to complicate matters, that had he not been shot, the man would likely have survived the fall as, unknown to him, a safety net had been erected below the second floor.

Given this new information, the medical examiner is sure that the death must be recorded as a homicide. But is he right?

A police investigation found that the shotgun had been fired by a man who lived with his wife in an apartment. Angry at his wife, he had gone to his desk for the gun, pointed it at her, and pulled the trigger. However, the shot missed the woman and, by a one-in-a-million chance, instead hit the tragic Ronald Opus as he fell outside their window.

Now normally, when a person intends to kill one human being and, by his action, kills another human being accidentally, the charge is still murder. But in this case, it turned out that there was yet another complication. Both the husband and wife told police, that they believed the gun was to be unloaded. The man had previously threatened his wife with an unloaded gun during arguments. The way the gun had become loaded was a total mystery, but the man was definitely not responsible. This evidence led the medical examiner to lean toward a new verdict: that of accidental death.

But what do you think?

Now the plot, which is fairly thick already, thickens. Further investigation, including fingerprint evidence, will solve the mystery of who loaded the gun. It turns out to be none other than the "falling man", Ronald Opus himself! Indeed, his diary reveals this plus the fact that he was angry at the woman and knew that the man often pretended to shoot her, and that he had loaded the firearm with the hope that the next time the two argued, the man would kill her. Given this new information, what should the medical examiner's verdict be?

Well, for what it's worth, Don Mills thinks Ronald's death should ultimately be ruled a suicide.

All right, it's a bit of a silly story. I find it a bit macabre too, but I can imagine it would have been great after the dinner speech to a convention of medical examiners. And yet, behind it, even for the rest of us, there is perhaps one important message. Which is that 'circumstances alter cases.' In this sense, the story offers another perspective, another insight, into the kinds of real-life interconnectivity and paradox that are often the unannounced ingredients of our jokes. Maybe it's not an 'Ah-ha!' moment, but it is certainly one more example of how humor can get you thinking.

Chapter 9
Making the Link between
Jokes and Creativity

Arthur Koestler visits an exhibition of cartoons. (By Eric Koch for Anefo)

The thing I most admire about witty people is not actually their being witty, but their ability to spark new ideas and make new connections. It's a difference that some stand-up comedians often inadvertently illustrate. Those who are good take their audience on wonderful tours of fantasy, jumping from one idea to the next, aided by a remarkable ability to summon up obscure information, while the less good rely on repetition and relentless obscenity. Likewise, the best comedians can take the jeers of hecklers and throw them back as ingenious or even devastating put-downs. The ones who are bad reply instead on aggression and obscenities, hoping to win the audience over with their "expertise" in breaking social taboos.

Hecklers matter. You need a few of them in a comedy club, and hecklers are, of course, part and parcel of politics. Many a political career has been won or lost after an off-the-cuff remark to a heckler caught on camera, as noted already in my discussion of American presidential wit. It's not that we actually think a 'good sense of humor' is necessary for a politician; we presumably would settle for competence and honesty, but it is because a GSOH seems to be an indicator of intelligence. Elon Musk, for example, regularly tweets material that has little purpose other than being a bit of a chuckle, for example, quipping that he always thought his name should be associated with a scandal 'Elon-gate.' Shortly after announcing his bid to buy Twitter, he said that his strategy was to make the site 'maximum fun.' For him, a site that churns out jokes is a site that is working. And for Musk, I suspect, the valuable thing about humor is its link to creativity.

However, let's go back to a rather serious book, entitled. *'The Act of Creation'* by Arthur Koestler, to explore this link. Koestler, who was born in Hungary but lived mostly in Britain, is best known for his novel *Darkness at Noon*[107], an anti-totalitarian work written in the run-up to the Second World War with the Moscow trials of purged Communist Party officials in the foreground, and the two glowering figures of Hitler and Stalin as an ominous backdrop. Since we're talking about creativity, it's maybe a little bit ironic that the title of his most successful book was the inspiration of the publisher, not Koestler himself. In fact, Koestler originally favored calling it 'The Vicious Circle' but the publisher instead made a novel and unexpected connection to the words of Job in the Bible: 'They meet with darkness in the daytime and grope in the noonday as in the night.'[108]

Anyway, for Koestler, humor is just part of a broader theory of creativity, but a very characteristic part. The core idea is that creativity can be compared to a funfair slot machine in the sense that, occasionally, among the whirling ideas of the mind, three elements significantly line up, and out pours the cash. The great thing about jokes and humor is that they give our brains the pleasure of connecting things of suddenly seeing the cherries line up. Put more grandly,

---

[107] Koestler,1940

[108] *The New Yorker,* September 23 2019

creativity emerges from the mind's pattern-recognition machinery and requires the synthesis of raw material into new ideas.

Koestler himself only ever worked as an author and journalist yet was deeply interested in all kinds of psychological and even paranormal phenomena. Nonetheless, his insights continue to be discussed in academic and expert circles to this day.

The contemporary Cambridge neuroscientist, Daniel Bor, for example, has also written about how built-in strategies for pattern recognition are essential to consciousness and our entire experience of life. In his book, *The Ravenous Brain: How the New Science of Consciousness Explains Our Insatiable Search for Meaning,* he says:

'The process of combining more primitive pieces of information to create something more meaningful is a crucial aspect both of learning and of consciousness and is one of the defining features of human experience. Once we have reached adulthood, we have decades of intensive learning behind us, where the discovery of thousands of useful combinations of features, as well as combinations of combinations and so on, has collectively generated an amazingly rich, hierarchical model of the world.'[109]

The point is, your mind consists of vast amounts of information, or data, if you prefer, which is indexed to a greater or lesser extent by rules and associations. You can't usually remember what you ate for dinner a year ago, but you just might if that date happens to be your birthday. And as Steve Jobs famously put it, 'creativity is just connecting things.'[110]

So, let's go back to Koestler's theory. He gives it a grand name: bisociation and draws some rather dull-looking diagrams to illustrate how he thinks ideas "bisociate", which it would not help to see, although evidently the written description leaves much to be desired. This runs:

"The pattern underlying [the creative act] is the perceiving of a situation or idea, L, in two self-consistent but habitually incompatible frames of reference, M1 and M2. The event L, in which the two intersect, is made to vibrate simultaneously on two different wavelengths, as it were. While this unusual situation lasts, L is not merely linked to one associative context but bisociated with two."[111]

---

[109] Bor 2012, 125

[110] *Wired* 1995

[111] Koestler 1940, 35

It's a complicated way to say something simple. Which is that with humor, as we've seen already in other theories, the fun comes from the clash between two competing terms of reference, each of which has, as Koestler says, its own logic and rules of the game. Put another way, "bisociation" is the "Ah-ha moment".

"Often these rules are implied, as hidden axioms, and taken for granted—the code must be de-coded. The rest is easy: find the 'link'—the focal concept, word, or situation that is bisociated with both mental planes; lastly, define the character of the emotive charge and make a guess regarding the unconscious elements that it may contain."

Take Elon Musk's pun, mentioned above: 'elongate/ Elon-gate.' Puns like this represent the bisociation of a single phonetic form with two meanings—two strings of thought tied together by an acoustic knot.

Koestler says that the popularity of such world games with children and in certain forms of mental disorder ('punning mania'), as well as in dreams, 'indicates the profound unconscious appeal of association based on pure sound.'

This mention of dreams brings us back to Sigmund Freud's writings and theories. Specifically, in explaining how a joke is formed, Freud makes a connection between the interplay between the conscious and unconscious, an interplay epitomized by words with two possible interpretations.

One example that Freud gives, which only works if you speak German, is that if a psychologist asks a youthful patient if they stimulate themselves sexually, the response might be 'ona, nie!' The joke for Freud comes from the dual role of the German word "nie", meaning on its own, "never", but also combining with "ona" to make "onanie", meaning "masturbation". Such sexual connections, of course, are deeply significant to us in Freud's view. However, double entendres and wordplay don't have to contain a sexual element to be attractive psychologically. Freud offers as another example the story of Hirsch-Hyacinth boasting of his relations with a wealthy individual, Baron Rothschild.

'And, as true as God shall grant me all good things, Doctor, I sat beside Salomon Rothschild, and he treated me quite as his equal—quite famillionairely'[112]

The, to my mind, rather feeble humor here comes from the creation of a compound word from the two words "familiarly" and "millionaire". Freud uses this joke as an example of the technique he calls "condensation". The technique of "double meaning" however, is explained with this joke:

'A doctor, as he came away from a lady's bedside, said to her husband with a shake of his head, "I don't like her looks." "I've not liked her looks for a long time," the husband hastened to agree.'[113]

It is an example of 'double meaning', with there being a tiny pun on the word 'looks'. But back to the secrets of the creative mind. In an essay for the magazine *Commentary* published in 1940, the year that Koestler's book first came out, the writer and poet Kathleen Nott says:

'The common pattern which Mr. Koestler discerns in original scientific discovery, in painting and music, in poetry and fiction, in both comedy and tragedy, can be seen at its most primitive in the anatomical structure of a joke.'

She chooses an example from the book, explaining that her choice is not because it is by any means the best joke (a venerable chestnut, as Mr. Koestler says, worn out by analysis), but because of its compactness.

A convict was playing cards with his jailers. On discovering that he cheated, they kicked him out of jail.

Indeed, it is a rather feeble joke, but then it is the structure that is offered as the important thing. Nott explains that for Koestler, it provides an example of a single sentence in which two conventional rules, 'offenders are punished by being locked up' and 'cheats are punished by being kicked out', each of them self-consistent, collide in a given situation.

---

[112] Freud 1922, 13
[113] Freud 1922, 37

This, then, is the "bisociational pattern" that Nott praises Koestler for managing to track down and illustrate, 'not only in the mind and works of man, but throughout the living universe.' Nott herself describes the theory like this:

"When two independent matrices of perception or reasoning interact with each other, the result... is either a collision ending in laughter, their fusion in a new intellectual synthesis, or their confrontation in an aesthetic experience... the same pair of matrices can produce comic, tragic, or intellectually challenging effects."

Or, put more simply, the emotional context is crucial to interpreting events. This is why the fat man slipping on the icy pavement can equally well become a comic or a tragic figure, depending on whether the spectator's attitude is dominated by malice or pity. And in between the two emotional extremes is what Nott calls "the emotionally balanced attitude of the physician," whose primary concern is to investigate. Certainly, doctors don't normally laugh when they ask patients to explain how they got their injuries!

All of which really only serves to illustrate that jokes flourish with a little bit of malice, struggle in a climate of concern, and perish under scientific scrutiny.

Which brings me to another joke. It appears in an essay entitled 'Solving for Pattern,' Howard Silverman, who among other fine things, has taught courses on thinking at the Pacific Northwest College of Art, follows up on what he calls Koestler's "logic of laughter" in *The Act of Creation*, with a joke that he attributes to John von Neumann, who, like Koestler, was both Jewish and from Budapest, Hungary.

Joke #31: Shmoedipus

Two women meet while shopping at the supermarket in the Bronx. One looks cheerful, the other depressed. The cheerful one inquires:

'What's eating you?'

'Nothing's eating me.'

'Death in the family?'

'No, God forbid!'

'Worried about money?'

'No...nothing like that.'

'Trouble with the kids?'

'Well, if you must know, it's my little Jimmy.'

'What's wrong with him, then?'

'Nothing is wrong. His teacher said he must see a psychiatrist.'

Pause. 'Well, well, what's wrong with seeing a psychiatrist?'

'Nothing is wrong. The psychiatrist thinks he may have an Oedipus complex.'

Pause. 'Well, well, Oedipus or Shmoedipus, I wouldn't worry so long as he's a good boy and loves his mamma.'

Okay, so how's this joke work? As much as it does (because, to be honest, I don't like the joke much, although the run-up is well done), it is because we are swiftly caught up in a narrative and await the end hungrily. Albeit, we may be left rather disappointed. A lot of jokes do that too!

Nonetheless, what emerges is a kind of play on words, one that relies on the knowledge that a boy with an Oedipus complex harbors a desire to kill his father and marry his mother.

For Koestler, however, the joke illustrates a "clash" between two "codes" of knowing[114]. There is a (perceived) scientific knowledge and familial identity. These "bisociative" clashes were, for him, the source of the humor.

Let's look a bit more deeply at Koestler's "two-guinea" term "bisociative". In his book, *The Act of Creation,* Koestler explains the "logic of laughter" as "the clash of two mutually incompatible codes, or associative contexts, which explodes the [narrative] tension."

For him, jokes like this illustrate how 'the emotional climate changes by gradual transitions from aggressive to neutral to sympathetic and *identifactory*— or, to put it another way, from an absurd through an abstract to a tragic or lyric view of existence.'

Another kind of creative thinking involves the ability to 'think sideways.' The contemporary comic, Ron Gifford, says that a sense of humor shows not only the ability to do this, but that it is a very useful kind of thinking skill. He says his favorite joke is that a skeleton goes into a bar and orders a drink and a mop...[115]

What's funny about that is people still thinking in straight lines will wonder. Well, the joke is that a skeleton "literally" can't hold his drink, so if he has one, it will spill out on the floor and need mopping up. Even with the

---

[114] Koestler 35

[115] Gifford 2013

joke explained, I don't find it funny, though. So, the fact that I didn't get it doesn't bother me so much—I was looking for something funny. Not something sad and weird and a little grotesque.

However, funny or not, for Gifford, it does show how "thinking sideways" involves making unusual and unexpected. connections. It is this, Gifford says, that is the key to creativity. As Edward de Bono once put it, 'creativity involves breaking out of established patterns in order to look at things in a different way.'[116]

A practical piece of advice Ron offers is that if you want to be funny, you have to make it into an everyday habit, not something you turn on and off. Humor should be an everyday habit, not just something used at dinner parties. Ron's strategy fits with something the American scientist, Linus Pauling once said, which is that the 'best way to have a good idea is to have a lot of ideas.'

That said, "eureka" insights in science, however desirable, cannot become everyday habits. As Koestler says, inevitably, as scientific insight becomes absorbed into a new normal, it loses its radicalism. Humor and artistic creativity, by contrast, retain something transitory; they belong to and encapsulate a moment in time and can be renewed too, for that reason.

In an article for Psychology Today, called 'The Power of Humor in Ideation and Creativity,' Moses Ma argues that the ability to acquire and process facts and observations—to reason—is fundamentally different from the ability to put them together in innovative ways. (Ma 2014) Well, we might have guessed this. But Moses has new evidence from Rex Jung, a researcher in neurosurgery at the University of New Mexico and a practicing neuropsychologist, that he thinks proves that creative capacities are not the same as intellectual capacities. Jung claims to be able to observe the differences via brain scans. He says that when people perform intellectual tasks, neural networks function in "directed and linear" ways.

On the other hand, when we attempt to perform more creative tasks, the neural pathways adopt more meandering and circumlocutory paths. Jung calls this alternative brain functioning transient hypofrontality, a term he uses to suggest that our usual neural process of seeing and processing the world switches off for a while to make space for a different kind of engagement.

---

[116] de Bono, 1

Jung sees the same process happening when creative people choose indirect strategies, such as going for a run or even meditating, to precipitate their best ideas. But having a laugh works even better! And indeed, nowadays, as Ma summarizes in the article, there's an entire branch of science called gelotology that studies the psychological and physiological effects of humor and laughter on the brain and the immune system. One thing researchers do agree on is that the cognitive mechanism behind humor and laughter is very complex.

For example, they point out in recent research[117] that EEG topographical brain mapping seems to show that the entire brain has to work together to appreciate a joke! First, the left hemisphere lights up as it begins to process the words, then the frontal lobe center of emotionality is activated before, milliseconds later, the right hemisphere starts processing the pattern, with just a few milliseconds later, the occipital lobe showing a spike in activity. A surge in delta waves marks the moment when the brain actually "gets the joke" (the researchers claim), after which the *nucleus accumbens* (a brain part involved in functions such as motivation, reward, or positive behavioral reinforcement) sends out positive signals, and finally, laughter erupts. Short version: the left hemisphere sets up the joke, and the right hemisphere "gets" it. Laughter, then, seems to be produced via a process that involves many regions of the brain.

Why is this? Well, researchers think that laughter represents a very fundamental, low-level form of communication—from limbic brain* to the limbic brain. It's a commonplace that people who relish each other's company laugh easily and often, whereas those who distrust or dislike each other laugh little, if at all. This is why laughter promotes bonding and team building.

Researchers are also finding that there are many other benefits to laughter and jokes. For example, it stimulates both sides of the brain to enhance learning by activating the limbic system in the brain* and connecting the right and left sides. Also, humor releases tension, which can lead to perceptual flexibility— a required component of creativity.

Studies have also found that dominant individuals, such as the boss of a company, or ambitious executives, use humor more than their subordinates. (For example, one academic study by Diane Martin concluded that organizational power/dominance and sex are better predictors of humor usage

---

[117] See, for example, Tian et al 2017

than other characteristic.'[118]) In such cases, controlling the laughter of a group can be a way of exercising power by directing the emotional state of the group. Steve Jobs' keynote speech launching the iPhone clocked in at one laugh every 100 seconds—better than most new comics!

Revealingly, however, it seems that as we age, and rather like Queen Victoria, we begin to lose our ability to be amused. A much-repeated claim (that seems to have no particular research base) is that children laugh four hundred times a day, while adults are lucky to have fifteen things to chuckle about. However, when Rod Martin looked more closely into it, he found that the surprisingly few studies in this area 'support the idea that adults and children show hugely different rates of laughter.'[119]

But the good news is that even though our brains inevitably lose the capacity to perform intellectual tasks as we age, partly because the covering that insulates neurons, called myelin, begins to physically deteriorate, the same process may actually aid creativity in that neural pathways begin to follow meandering paths. Perhaps within this, adds Moses Ma wryly, lies 'the punchline of life.'

*The limbic system of the brain is a group of structures that govern emotions and behavior. The limbic system, and in particular the hippocampus and amygdala, is involved in the formation of long-term memory and is closely associated with the olfactory structures (having to do with the sense of smell).

[118] See Martin et al 2004

[119] Martin, R., no date

Chapter 10
Men, Women and Smutty Jokes

"Full Frontal" with Samantha Bee was a U.S. late-night talk and satire show that aired on TBS from 2016 to 2022.

Warning! This chapter contains highly explicit jokes with female victims. But we still have to go here because, as Freud writes, wit is a form of sexual exhibition.

This is how Freud puts it:

'Wherever wit is not a means to its end, i.e., harmless, it puts itself in the service of but two tendencies which may themselves be united under one viewpoint; it is either hostile wit serving as aggression, satire, or defense, or it is obscene wit serving as a sexual exhibition.'[120]

---

[120] **Chapter 10** Freud 1922, 138

The philosophical literature on jokes and humor is there, but sparse. This is why Freud's book, devoted solely to the subject, is so important. Yet why would a serious investigator of human psychology spend so much time looking at jokes and wit? Well, in Freud's case anyway, it seems interest in humor may have been sparked by his own recollections of having been embarrassed by his father, who liked to tell vulgar jokes.

Freud calls jokes involving sex 'smutty.' He takes it all very literally, writing,

'The smutty joke is like the denudation of a person of the opposite sex toward whom the joke is directed. Through the utterance of obscene words, the person attacked is forced to picture the parts of the body in question, or the sexual act, and it is shown that the aggressor himself pictures the same thing. There is no doubt that the original motive of the smutty joke was the pleasure of seeing the sexuality displayed.'[121]

And surely Freud is recalling his own embarrassment when he says that the "smutty joke" makes "a confederate of the third person" by 'giving him pleasure through the utterance which causes the woman to be ashamed in his presence.'[122]

Earlier on, in *Wit and Its Relation to the Unconscious*, Freud wrote:

'One of the primitive components of our libido is the desire to see sexual exposure. Perhaps this itself is a development—a substitution for the desire to touch, which is assumed to be the primary pleasure.' [123]

It is this ability to offer substitute sexual pleasure through words that makes them such good business for stand-up comedians, blokes in bars (though not for university lecturers), and doubly rentable, as another aspect of this kind of humor is that:

'In all obscene jokes, we succumb to striking mistakes of judgment about the "goodness" of the joke as long as it depends upon formal conditions; the technique of these jokes is often very poor while their laughing effect is enormous.'[124]

Jokes that have a lot of laughing power and don't need to be clever clearly beat clever ones in the marketplace. If fashions change in public humor (and I

---

[121] Freud 1922, 140

[122] Freud 1922, 203–4

[123] Freud 1922, 141

[124] Freud 1922, 147-8

stress "public" as Trump's joshing in the locker room about his sexual conquests (see Chapter 2) shows there's a different kind of humor allowed outside the public eye), it's worth noting that for many years comedians dined out on a menu of jokes about mother-in-laws, silly wives, and big busted blondes. These were jokes told by men, for men, and the equivalent doesn't seem to exist either then or now with feminist comedians.

So, another way to look at Freud, though, is to say that he himself is presenting a "male" perspective on humor. After all, he traces much of it back to hate and sex, where an alternative approach, which women might claim is distinctively feminine, might emphasize the social aspect of jokes and the importance of shared humor in cementing relationships. Of course, jokes can not only bring men and women together, but they can also divide them too. As Schopenhauer says:

'That sexual relationships afford the easiest material jokes, always ready to hand, and accessible even to the feeblest wit, as is shown by the frequency of obscene jokes, could not be [the] case if deepest seriousness did not lie directly at their ground.'[125]

But, to make sense of smutty jokes, let's first of all talk about gender differences in humor *production* and look at more contemporary instances of women being witty, something Schopenhauer's known interest in concerned a certain seamstress who annoyed him by laughing and chattering outside his door, leading to a very disgraceful physical clash that saw the lady injured and Schopenhauer paying her a stipend for the rest of her life.

Academics have labored for many years to pinpoint the differences between the male and female styles of humor. But perhaps it is the British "funny-woman", Helen Lederer, whose television credits include the comedy series *Naked Video* and *Absolutely Fabulous*, who has offered the key insight when she once pointed out that there is an almost "authoritarian" aspect to joke-telling—everyone has to listen attentively to the joke, or they will miss key elements, and worst of all, come the punchline, you have to laugh, or seem stupid, or to have no sense of humor (or both).

As Lederer puts it:

'When a man tells a formalized joke, I tend to switch off because it's quite authoritarian: you have to listen in order to get the payoff, the punchline, and

---

[125] Schopenhauer, 112

then you have to laugh. It's quite strict and inflexible. It's far more interesting for me to ramble on, hopefully hitting the right targets, certainly with a throughline, and certainly with an end, but not in the same formalized way. I would rather just sit and hope that it's funny.'[126]

This 'hold the floor and ramble on' aspect is very true and doesn't apply just to formal jokes. I was watching a British funny program called *Have I Got News for You* the other day, which is, superficially, a kind of panel quiz about recent news events but really a vehicle for the four panelists (invariably there are three men and one woman) to offer quips and one-liners. Here, (just as we all might find in a conversation), to intervene in fast banter with witticism or one-line comments involves a certain power-play. In fact, many episodes of the show have the "guest" panelists barely speaking while the regulars are quipping away, so to speak, and yet, wit is also something of a great equalizer on shows like this, just as it can be at parties or even mealtimes.

A previously rather meek guest can stop the flow and have everyone laughing with them with a well-placed observation. Likewise, as teachers and lecturers know, if someone in their class makes a witty observation or makes a humorous comparison, the class laughs with the joker, despite the hierarchy being firmly fixed in favor of the teacher. (Hopefully, the teacher laughs too.)

Laughter like this is:

'a slight revolt on the surface of social life…a froth with a saline base. Like froth, it sparkles…But the philosopher who gathers a handful to taste may find that the substance is scanty and the aftertaste bitter.' (Henri Bergson, *La Rire*[127])

At this point, let's have a joke—a sexist one—to bear in mind.

Joke # 32: The Spurned Blonde

A pretty, young blonde woman is shocked to find out that her husband is having an affair and goes to a gun shop to buy a handgun. The next day, she comes home and confronts her husband in bed with a beautiful redhead. She takes out the gun and holds it to her own head. The husband jumps out of bed, begging and pleading with her not to shoot herself. Hysterically, the blonde responds to the husband, 'Shut up! You're next!'

---

[126] Goodman 1992, 295
[127] Bergson 1911, 61a-61b

A bitter aftertaste is particularly evident with "sexist" jokes. This highlights the fact that, as Freud writes, a joke is a double-dealing rascal who serves two masters: the joke teller and the audience—who both mock the target identified in the joke.

Henri Bergson's perspective is a little more nuanced. He says that laughter is, above all, a corrective.

"Being intended to humiliate, it must make a painful impression on the person against whom it is directed. With laughter, society avenges itself for the liberties taken with it. It would fail in its object if it bore the stamp of sympathy or kindness."[128]

Pause a moment here, to recall what happened in 2010 when Daniel Tosh, a white male comedian, made a "rape joke" at a "Laugh Factory" show, the gist of which was that rape jokes were always funny. Tosh's style is to be "sarcastic", so other jokes included a skit about slavery having been "a pretty cool trick" on account of black people having had, but not used, certain physical advantages. The skit, like the rape joke one, was, of course, controversial. But more controversial still was that, when he was called out by a woman in the audience, he ad-libbed by asking the room, 'Wouldn't it be funny if that girl got raped by, like, five guys right now? Like right now? What if a bunch of guys were just raped here?'

The remark led to accusations that Tosh was making light of rape or, in the words of El Hut, in *I-d Magazine*, that he had removed the tragedy and pain from a gravely serious crime—totally misusing the power that he holds onstage as a man holding a microphone[129]. Indeed, it is quite hard to see the remarks as a joke. They seem to lack the surely essential element of a joke, which is some kind of clever twist or hidden subtlety. Nonetheless, Tosh's words were seen by most of the audience as hilarious, and few—if any—walked out. Henri Bergson explains what might otherwise seem like an inexplicable appreciation of off-color jokes; thus, when he writes that laughter:

'…cannot be absolutely just. Nor should it be kind-hearted either. Its function is to intimidate by humiliating. Now, it would not succeed in doing this had nature not been implanted for that very purpose, even in the best of men, a spark of spitefulness or, at all events, of mischief. Perhaps we had better not investigate this point too closely, for we should not find anything very

---

[128] Bergson 1911, 60a-60b

[129] I-*d Magazine* 2018

flattering to ourselves. We should see that this movement of relaxation or expansion is nothing but a prelude to laughter, that the laugher immediately retires within himself, more self-assertive and conceited than ever, and is evidently disposed to look upon another's personality as a marionette of which he pulls the strings. In this presumptuousness, we speedily discern a degree of egoism and, behind this latter, something less spontaneous and more bitter—the beginnings of a curious pessimism, which becomes more pronounced as the *laugher* more closely analyzes his *laughter*.'[130]

Bergson allows that jokes may be sexist, indeed that they may be obviously so, and yet what is going on is much more complicated, more universal, and more interesting psychologically.

What sort of "psychological differences" might there be? Many academic studies have come to different conclusions. However, a few years ago (in 2020), researchers Jennifer Hofmann and colleagues saved us a lot of bother when they came up with a review of many studies into 'Gender differences in humor-related traits, humor appreciation, production, comprehension, (neural) responses, use, and correlates.' After reviewing "all available peer-reviewed literature on humor and gender differences" between 1977–2018, they identified seven kinds of "psychological" gender differences in humor[131].

First of all, men have more aggressive "humor styles" and 'men obtain higher scores on katagelasticism.' [132] "Katagelasticism", by the way, is a word that really isn't helpful to use. It's not even useful for Scrabble. It means 'the joy of laughing at others.'

Secondly, they found that 'Gender differences exist for the appreciation of sexual humor,' with men targeting women and women targeting men. Who would have expected that?

On the other hand (this is their third point), where the jokes were essentially "nonsense", no gender differences appeared.

Their fourth finding, in the classic "more research needed" researcher style, was that studies were split between whether men or women are funnier. On the fifth question of whether men and women are equally able to appreciate a joke, the studies seemed to agree that this ability is at least equally shared among the population.

---

[130] Bergson 1911, 61a

[131] Hofmann, 1

[132] Hofman, 11

A sixth finding was that 'in terms of humor use,' or how jokes are told, gender differences emerged but seemed to reflect 'gender roles rather than natural differences.' Specifically, that, 'When exposed to humor stimuli, different neural responses of men and women in prefrontal cortex activations (or selected parts) were found.'

And point seven, looking at gender roles, was that women typically valued humor production abilities more than humor receptivity, while for men, women's receptivity to their own humor was more important than the woman's humor production abilities.

The researchers closed with the recommendation that attention should be paid to disentangling actual gender differences from gender role expectations and gender stereotypes, and the warning that self-reporting may accentuate roles and stereotypes.

Nonetheless, superficially, it does seem that there are underlying gender differences in humor. Both in "production" telling jokes, and in consumption, listening to and appreciating them. Put another way, it seems that there are things that blokes laugh about with their mates and different things gals giggle about at parties. (Sexism intended.)

And it seems that men dominate "laughter production", leaving women only the subordinate role of an appreciative audience. Lizbeth Goodman, a researcher who describes herself as a specialist in 'working with people who do not have physical voices' has 'wondered why it was that when a man tells a joke and women don't laugh, we are told we have no sense of humor, but when a woman tells a joke and men don't laugh, we are told we are not funny.'[133]

Yet little is entirely straightforward in humor research. When Eric Bressler, Rod Martin, and Sigal Balshine (2006) thought they had found that "men and women may think that men are funnier" (the attribution bias was replicated in different studies), they immediately qualified the finding by saying 'whether they actually are funnier is to be debated.'[134]

Twenty or so years ago, a study by Martina Lampert and Susan Ervin-Tripp (1998) attempted to bring together and summarize the state of the art of literature on gender and the sense of humor. They concluded that men use more humor than women, men oddly appreciate humor more than women, especially

---

[133] Jenkins,1985, 135

[134] Bressler 2016, 23

aggressive and sexual humor, and both genders display more humor directed at female than male targets. They also found that both 'men and women enjoy jokes about sexual relationships and sometimes tell similar jokes, but their jokes do not serve the same psychological or interpersonal functions.'

Another, much cited study that does offer a firm claim for gender differences in the "consumption side" of jokes is by Thomas Herzog (1999). Herzog comes to two apparently firm conclusions. First, because females dislike jokes with female victims, 'females uniformly dislike female victimization, regardless of explicitness.' This is tautological, of course. His second finding is that males prefer "sexual" over "hostile" jokes and "high" to "low" explicitness.

Even this meager evidence is disputed by other researchers. A study by Van Giffen and Maher (1995) "found that when participants recalled humorous incidents from their lives that did not involve jokes or prepared humor, the most prevalent theme was not sex or hostility but stupidity."

Perhaps at this point we should step back and look at what sort of jokes the researchers are using when carrying out their humor tests for gender differences. In Van Giffen and Maher's study, the cartoons were things like this:

Picture: A naked man and woman seated at the edge of the bed, the man covering his genitals with his hands, the woman holding a ruler, and the woman speaking.

Caption: 'Come on, it's only for my diary.'

This was counted as 'highly explicit.'

An example of a cartoon with what the researchers classified as a "female sexual victim" and "low explicitness" was this.

Picture: A man speaking to a woman at a party.

Caption: 'How would you like to come up to my place and see my silver memorial coins of famous women in history?'?

Here's a last example of a "hostile" joke. It is categorized as having a "female victim" and "low explicitness".

Picture: Man and woman seated in the living room, woman looking displeased and man looking pleased, man speaking.

Caption: 'I just said that for comic effect.'

There are a lot of subtle assumptions being made. Likewise, I think the cartoonists here are all men. I don't know, but the point is, it's not explicitly stated, as it's assumed not to matter.

Given that, and more generally, how complicated it all seems, wouldn't it be wonderful if there was a way to look inside people's heads and see how jokes actually work in real time? Humble folk might think this is a nice idea but hopefully impractical, but just fancy that! In recent years, researchers have been using brain scans and MRNI imaging to try to do just this. One study attempting this kind of thing by Yu-Chen Chan, Yi-Jun Liao, Cheng-Hao Tu, and Hsueh-Chih Chen found that:

'...results showed that women exhibited greater cerebral activity in the temporo-parietal-mesiocortical-motor cortcx than men while processing the jokes in general. Also, women showed greater activity in the fronto-mesolimbic network while processing "exaggeration jokes" compared to men. "Ambiguity jokes" elicited greater cerebral activity in the frontal paralimbic network in men as compared to women. All joke types elicited greater activation in the anterior prefrontal gyrus of women than in those of men, whereas men showed greater activation than women in the dorsal prefrontal cortex.'[135]

Note how the "categories" of humor are freely added to the speculative mix.

Another study, in the same spirit, by Yi-Tzu Chang, Li-Chuan Ku, and Hsueh-Chih Chen, using their own three-stage model of 'incongruity detection, incongruity resolution, and elaboration' stages, found that women "recruited more mental resources" to integrate cognitive and emotional components at the final stage. In contrast, men 'recruited more automated processes during the transition from the cognitive operations of the incongruity resolution stage to the emotional response of the humor elaboration stage.' This all demonstrated, the authors thought, that sex differences in humor processing lay in differences in 'the integration of cognitive and emotional components, which are closely linked and interact reciprocally, particularly in women.'[136]

Such research is imprcssivc to ordinary folks, yet there are good reasons to be skeptical. That well-informed questioner, Raymond Tallis, author of a book

---

[135] Chan 2016
[136] Chang 2018

called *Aping Mankind*, summarizes many of them. For a start, he reminds us 'that most brain activity is not associated with consciousness, and the small part that is associated does not look all that different from the large amount that is not.' The broader point, he elaborates, is that 'the more you think about the idea that human life can be parceled out into discrete functions that are allocated to their own bits of the brain, the more absurd it seems.'[137]

Tallis says that we need to reconsider that puzzling phenomenon "consciousness" because, as Descartes pointed out all those years ago, the only thing we can really be sure of is that we are conscious. If we are at a comedy club looking at a show, it is possible, if unlikely, that the whole show might be a hologram or that we are not really there but dreaming of it. But the fact that you "think" you are at the show cannot be denied, as long as you are thinking about it. This is how Tallis puts it in his book:

'Physicalist neuroscience has no problem with light getting into the brain through the eyes and triggering impulses. Looking out at the gaze is another matter entirely.'

And a bit later, he adds, 'It is a person that looks out, not a brain.' [138]

Philosophers stress that the world is an undifferentiated mass until the mind splits it up into discrete parts.

Even neurophysiologists allow that the object that we construct is not really there but created by the brain. Yet there is something paradoxical: the brain is shaping the world that it is shaped by. Tallis offers this metaphor: '…think of everyday consciousness as a million sets of ripples in a pond created by the impact of a dense shower of hail, compounded by all sorts of internal sources of ripples. Ultimately, the nervous system has to allow everything to merge in the moment of present consciousness.'[139]

Tallis thinks that several things have slipped the philosophers by in their enthusiasm for the latest brain research, notably that 'the physical world does not have tensed time, in which present, past, and future exist.' This is a creation of consciousness. And alongside that, the notion of "position" is an uncomfortable one to apply to a nerve impulse, which is a signal that never stops moving and never arrives.

---

[137] Tallis 2011, 82
[138] Tallis 2011, pages 105 and 109
[139] Tallis 2011, 122

Put large, Tallis is appalled by what he calls the 'Darwinization of our understanding of humanity.'[140] as well as "neuromania", which he defines as the almost ubiquitous use of what is offered as the latest, cutting-edge brain science to supposedly reveal how our minds work.

His antidote to errors created by such thinking is to remind us that there is a difference between "brain activity" and consciousness. Tallis says he started arguing at this point as a medical student and has been struggling to communicate it ever since.

Which is why, in *Aping Mankind*, he first of all, briefly and competently, explains that the brain simply cannot be reduced to a computer, impressive though today's computers are.

First, Tallis accuses the experiments of being laughably crude and mind-numbingly simplistic. In one experiment, care assistants were asked to look at photos of people with intellectual disabilities first in a neutral way and secondly, 'with a feeling of unconditional love.' No, really! In other, more conventional experiments, subjects are exposed to different stimuli, and the change in brain activity is recorded. Thus, subjects may be shown photographs of friends on the one hand and lovers on the other, and the "differences" in the brain scans taken to indicate the "unconditional love" spot. Tallis is scathing, pointing out that even in more mundane experiments in which subjects were asked to, for example, tap their fingers, 'the test-retest correlation ranged between 0.76 and zero!'[141] In other words, nothing could be deduced from the brain scans about finger-tapping. How much less can be deduced about complex intellectual and emotional reactions to things like jokes?

But it is his second line of attack that is perhaps more deadly. Tallis writes that the 'seemingly unlimited power of computers to do things detect events, "calculate", "control" outputs,' make it superficially attractive to 'think of the mind-brain as a computer, and an enormously powerful one.' But Tallis says that the mind is non-linear and "also unified" whereas computers are linear, necessarily modular, and fragmentary. Nor, he adds, is it any more persuasive to make the computer out of a vast array of molecules, as Francis Crick imagined when he wrote:

---

[140] Tallis 2011, 5
[141] Tallis 2011, 77

'You, your joys and sorrows, your memories and your ambitions, our sense of personal identity and free will, are in fact no more than the behavior of a vast assembly of nerve cells and their associated molecules.'

Tallis recalls Crick's phrase in his book, but it is in his own words that he argues:

'You would have to be pretty resistant to the overwhelming body of evidence to deny that the human brain is an evolved organ, fashioned by the processes of natural selection acting on spontaneous variation. It does not follow from this that the mind is unless you believe that the mind is identical with brain activity.'[142]

To cut a long story short, even if male and female brains work differently, it is quite a jump to claim that there are "male and female" minds, and still, yet another to suppose that they process jokes differently.

It seems much more likely, and this is one point that most researchers agree on is that "gender differences" are, in reality, socially imposed stereotypes. To which end, Jennifer Hofmann and collaborators saved us a lot of bother a few years ago when they came up with a review of many studies into 'Gender differences in humor-related traits, humor appreciation, production, comprehension, (neural) responses, use, and correlates.' Central among their findings was that:

'Some differences may be explicitly linked to certain gender roles and cultural specifics (such as cultural display rules, politeness norms, etc.), that do not relate to actual differences between men and women, but rather norms and roles that are carried out.'[143]

The same idea was investigated in a study by Andrew Schwehm, Wilson McDermut, and Katherine Thorpe (2015), when they claimed to have found that female comedians had higher scores in neuroticism. Put another way, even if the "technical problems" and the contaminating confusion of a myriad social norms can be overcome with such research, the conceptual chasm remains.

For all such reasons, I propose at this point to abandon complicated ways to identify gender differences in humor and instead explore much more simple and straightforward avenues of investigation. For example, look at the humor styles of a clutch of recent well-known wits.

---

[142] Tallis 2011, 43

[143] Hofmann 2020

Let's start with what might be considered a couple of "case studies", and a peek at the list of what the Webber, "ScrollDroll", calls the most famous comedians of "history", but the list is, in reality, limited to the last decade or so.

Published in 2022, ScrollDroll's list of the '18 Best Stand-Up Comedians in the World Who Make You Laugh Out Loud'[144] is overwhelmingly male. If their list is representative, then it seems that, in humor, as in most things (according to men), men are best! Can this be right? Especially when things like "relationships" are a significant theme for many of the comics? Bear with me for the next few pages, if I start "listing slightly", to use a word in a confusing way, as so much comedy does. The purpose of these lists is to enable you, the reader, to see the "evidence", rather than just have me select the bits that fit my own view and serve it up on a plate. Here, I want to test two selections other people have made of recent, highly successful (U.S.) comics to see whether there is a distinctively male kind of 'humor production' (content) or a distinctively male style of delivery.

So, let's see. Introducing our first sample, the ScrollDroll list, Simran Marthas says, 'Every comedian has a distinct set of skills, genres, life experiences, and a unique approach to pitching jokes.' And straight off, clearly, the life experiences of women, from the standpoint of comedy, are not considered significantly different from those of men.

Next, let's take a look at the list and see which topics are featured. Proudly wearing the laurels at No. 1 is Louis CK, or Louis Alfred Székely, to give him his real name. Louis CK's jokes are 'about making us look in the mirror and face our insecurities and embarrassments, and then going one step further to build the courage to laugh at them.' Note the inclusive pronouns. The CK brand seems to transcend gender.

But that's just being hinted at here. ScrollDroll says directly of its Number 2, Bill Blur, that he not only transcends gender issues but appropriates them for comedic purposes. 'His no-holds-barred approach to issues such as feminism, gender equality, and religion frequently lands him in hot water, but it is precisely this quality that distinguishes him in the ever-increasing climate of political correctness.'

---

[144] ScrollDroll 2022

Coming in at Number 3 is Amy Schumer, who 'broke through to the big time in comedy via acting.' Amy has a stand-up routine that offers 'a uniquely female perspective on past and present relationships,' while also 'having the potential to be dark at times.' This would seem to be a promising seam to investigate, but being only a humble website, ScrollDroll offers no further detail on what exactly is "unique" about Amy's approach to gender and humor.

And so on to Number 4, who is Dave Chappelle, whose fame stems partly from his success at Comedy Central or "arguably" even more from his "walking away" from it. Chappelle, we are told, 'embraces brutal honesty when it comes to race, sexuality, and American culture.' So, again, apparently, a male comic is able to transcend his own gender.

Number 5. Jerry Seinfeld, of 1990s sitcom fame, freely, and again, presumably, gender neutrally, picks up on 'on the most absurd details from day-to-day life.'

Number 6. Chris Rock is credited here for comedy material that crisscrosses three areas: politics, American race relations, and (of most interest to us) the male-woman relationship.

So far, this humble case study suggests that gender issues are comedic material available equally to both male and female comics.

However, the next three on the list are Kevin Hart and Eddie Murphy, well-known for their films but who began their careers as stand-up comedians, and Robin Williams, another movie star who also started out as a stand-up comedian. They are not credited here with any gender-linked material, politically correct or otherwise.

Quite a contrast then with Number 10, which is another woman, Tig Notaro, who (we are told) has been doing stand-up since the early 2000s and appeared on shows such as *Comedy Central Presents* and *The Sarah Silverman Show*. But here's the thing ScrollDroll highlights: in 2012, Tig announced on stage at one of her shows that she had been diagnosed with breast cancer 'and discussed her other personal issues.' Fellow comedian Louis C. K. and a slew of other renowned comedians present that night dubbed the set 'one of the greatest stand-up performances ever.' What's more, when she put the audio of the show on iTunes, it went to No. 1 on Billboard's Top Comedy Albums chart! To the extent that such popular rankings really count, then it looks like comedy material about women's issues (narrowly defined) is best done by…women.

Or is it? Number 11 is Mike Birbiglia, a comic known for long-form jokes, usually in the form of stories and anecdotes delivered deadpan, 'that build up to a big finish.' ScrollDroll says that his material is "deeply personal," drawing heavily on his "life experiences and relationships". Birbiglia also found success with a Netflix comedy special called "My Girlfriend's Boyfriend", which aired in 2013, to positive reviews.

Jim Gaffigan comes in at number 12, and while there are more, this should suffice for our sampling purposes. Jim began stand-up in the late 1980s and has been dubbed the "everyman" comedian because his material is 'largely observational, clean, and revolves around topics that are easily relatable, with a strong focus on food and parenting.' Yes, *parenting*!

Okay, accepting that each of these people 'have the ability to make you laugh so hard that you will clutch your stomach and beg them to stop' (*Hmmm),* and there's apparently a significant amount of what we might call 'gender-neutral' observation humor.

Not convinced? Well, here, again chosen (more or less) at random, is another list, another "case study". This time it is 'The Nine Best Late-Night TV Hosts Currently on Air,' as ranked by Shawn Van Horn[145] And straight off, note that there's a proportion of eight males to one female, a discrepancy that again either suggests men are basically funnier than women or that there's a lot of sexism in the humor business. In descending order of funniness, this time, they are:

Jimmy Fallon, of *The Tonight Show,* at Number 9. Fallon apparently has the 'annoying habit of laughing too often when there's not even a joke, and there's no bite to his comedy.' 'Still, if you prefer a simpler monologue and fun games, a good time can be found.' Anyway, for our purposes, he seems not to major on gender.

However, Number 8. Samantha Bee certainly does. Her late-night talk and news satire show, *Full Frontal with Samantha Bee,* aired on TBS from 2016 to 2022. The only woman of the bunch showcases 'a woman's perspective on the day's news, while also highlighting women's issues that her male colleagues couldn't do justice to' this according to Shawn Van Horn. He adds that her approach has been a success at times, but that her 'more angry style' has led to criticism. Shawn thinks that some of that 'has come from

---

[145] Collider.com 2022

misogynistic expectations of how a woman should act,' but some has indeed been brought on herself, such as when she called Ivanka Trump a 'feckless c*nt.'

Let's move on quickly to Number 7. Trevor Noah, of *The Daily Show*. Noah, we are told, speaks from the outsider's view as someone from the other side of the world, while also tapping into how Millennials and Gen Z look at issues. But there's apparently no great emphasis on anything gender related.

Number 6. James Corden, of *The Late Show,* is known for his Carpool Karaoke segments, which involve him driving around town singing with the world's top singers, in the process piling up millions of views on YouTube and becoming very rich. I checked the guest list, so to speak, and it seems Corden prefers chatting to ladies, but that doesn't seem to be because he thinks they are funnier; rather, it seems to fit the stereotype of women being good audiences for male (Corden's) wit.

At Number 5 is one of my favorite Late Night hosts, Jimmy Kimmel, who has hosted his own ABC show since 2003. Don't come here for "smutty jokes" about women; instead, the former star of "The Man Show" has evolved his act from 'a more immature sense of humor to something that, while still funny, can also be very serious.' Several times, we are told, Kimmel has shed tears on camera, including about his young son's health. Kimmel, we might say, transcends the male stereotype. Other popular segments are just gender-neutral, such as 'This Week in Unnecessary Censorship' and 'Celebrities Read Mean Tweets.'

Number 4 is Seth Meyers, whose years of co-hosting *Weekend Update* with Tina Fey (who doesn't get a look-in here) led him to the world of late nights and eventual success with his "A Closer Look" segments. In these, similar to what Jon Stewart did every night on *The Daily Show* or what John Oliver still does every Sunday, Meyers picks a subject in the news and attempts to dissect it while being humorous. Such sketches are essentially political, and gender issues are marginal.

Number 3, Daniel Baker and Joel Martinez, are described as 'the new kids on the block,' with a show offering a black and Latino perspective. 'These two guys, sitting in relaxing chairs and clad in whatever clothes they were wearing when they left the house, could be any of us, simply riffing on life,' says Van Horn, perhaps rather too quickly, including women in his assessment.

Number 2 is John Oliver, whose show is *Last Week Tonight.* Again, Van Horn insists that 'the viewer,' that gender-neutral creature, is guaranteed not only to laugh but to learn a lot as well. Having watched Oliver at work, I know that his fact-based, political humor involves a lot of vulgar asides, which Freud would not have approved of, but for Van Horn, the great thing about the show is that it 'lets the issues linger in our psyche.'

And finally, Number 1, which is Stephen Colbert of *The Late Show.*

The 'leader of the pack in ratings,' a late-night powerhouse from *The Daily Show,* and the Emmy-winning *Colbert Report.* Colbert's schtick is to be a 'nightly voice of reason.' He can 'joke around with the best of them,' but it's his 'serious discussions with journalists and those in the know, as well as his heartfelt talks with the likes of President Biden and Andrew Garfield about their shared loss, that make Colbert the best in the game.'

Well, whatever the truth or otherwise of all this, let's just notice how "gender-neutral" the themes and topics are for the men, while the routines of the sole women on the list highlight…gender issues. What this quick tour of recent American comedy indicates to me is that humor (wit) is very much a male-dominated sport. However, and perhaps less obviously, it also suggests that the material, the jokes, are not particularly sexist, not a form of male sexual display as Freud intimated, but rather reflect more liberal and often egalitarian ideas and themes. Put short: jokes are not sexist; people are.

Chapter 11
Dark Comedy

Dr. Strangelove—The War Room

I'll never forget my granddad's last words to me just before he died. "Are you still holding the ladder?"

Freud called it tendentious wit. But we know it better as dark comedy or black comedy. Or gallows humor. The kind of wit where the condemned man on the gallows asks, 'Are you sure this thing is safe?' But whatever you call it, dark comedy consists of jokes that make fun of ordinarily taboo subjects. Taboos are funny. Take cannibalism, for example. In the otherwise by-turns violent and creepy film *The Silence of the Lambs*, audiences regularly laugh when Hannibal Lecter bids naive young thing Clarice a suave farewell: 'I do wish we could chat longer, but I'm having an old friend for dinner.'

Topics tackled "humorously" in clubs, in YouTube videos, or in magazines these days may include:

- Murder, violence, and death
- Political corruption
- Human sexuality
- Poverty, disease, and famine
- Racial or sexual stereotypes

Of course, all these themes can also appear in less pointed form as elements of "ordinary comedy" too. But take jokes about death as a starting point. Is death funny? Is it ever a proper subject for jokes? Well, hold off on delivering a witty oration at the next funeral you attend, but the attitudes in the West toward this, ahem, most natural of human activities, are far from inevitable. Which is why, in ancient times, funerals were not solemn affairs, with people trudging to a graveyard to see a coffin; rather, they involved feasting, drunkenness, and not a little ribaldry.

In fact, for the Greeks in particular, death and having fun were closely linked. There were special funeral games that even extended to displays of crude sexual acts. Clay models of phalluses as well as obscene jokes served the same function: the regeneration and empowerment of life forces. Curiously, this link between death and feasting has been passed down the ages in our word "culinary," as the ethnographer, Lada Stevanović, points out. The word comes from *culina*, the place where a meal sacrifice was offered to the dead.[146]

But back to the present, and recent examples of jokes about people dying include:

- Jonathan Swift's essay, *A Modest Proposal,* which satirically urged the Irish to solve their economic problems by selling their children to the wealthy as food.
- *Weekend at Bernie's,* originally a book, later a film, whose plot revolves around two youngsters trying to make people believe a dead man is still alive.
- Monty Python's film, *Life of Brian*, which ends with a group of crucifixion victims singing, "Always Look on the Bright Side of Life."

---

[146] Stevanovic 2007

In a 2006 poll for British television station Channel 4, *Life of Brian* was ranked first on their list of the 50 Greatest Comedy Films ever. So here's a taste of its surreal humor: This scene, which begins the post-title action, has a crowd listening to Jesus/Brian speaking.

Joke #33: Life of Brian

GREGORY *(Trying to listen to the Sermon on the Mount)*:
Could you be quiet, please?
JESUS *(In the far distance)*:
They shall have the earth…
GREGORY:
What was that?
JESUS:
…for their possession. How blest are those…
MR. CHEEKY:
I don't know. I was too busy talking to Big Nose.
JESUS:
…who hunger and thirst to see…
MAN #1:
I think it was 'Blessed are the cheesemakers.'
JESUS:
…right prevail.
MRS. GREGORY:
Ahh, what's so special about the cheesemakers?
GREGORY:

Well, obviously, this is not meant to be taken literally. It refers to any manufacturer of dairy products.

However, for me, it is Stanley Kubrick's film *Dr. Strangelove, or How I Learned to Stop Worrying and Love the Bomb,* which is a classic example of comedy playing with life and death themes. The plot, very simply, is about the President's unsuccessful efforts to stop an unhinged United States Air Force general from launching a first-strike nuclear attack on the Soviet Union. Timeless stuff! The film ends with Dr. Strangelove leaping from his wheelchair and exclaiming, '*Mein Fuhrer,* I can walk again!' followed by a montage of bombs exploding to the wartime tune of 'We'll Meet Again.'

It is perhaps revealing that Kubrick had originally planned to end the film with everyone in the War Room involved in a classic comedic *finale*—a custard pie fight. Accounts vary as to why the pie fight scene was cut, but in a 1969 interview, Kubrick said, 'I decided it was a farce and not consistent with the satirical tone of the rest of the film.' Put another way, it was comedy, but not *dark* comedy.

The film came out in 1964, in the middle of the so-called "Cold War" conflict between the United States and the Soviet Union. It was based on a novel called *Red Alert* by Peter George that had been published six years earlier and was also about the threat of nuclear war. The book, however, is deadly serious and certainly offers nothing like a "Doctor Strangelove" character.

When the American Film Institute made a list of the 500 funniest films in 2000, *Strangelove* was right up there—listed as number three. But to me, it is not so much funny as so exquisitely, well, "dark".

Joke #34: The Survival Kit

'Survival kit contents check. In them you'll find: one forty-five caliber automatic; two boxes of ammunition; four days' concentrated emergency rations; one drug issue containing antibiotics, morphine, vitamin pills, pep pills, sleeping pills, and tranquilizer pills; one miniature combination Russian phrase book and Bible; one hundred dollars in rubles; one hundred dollars in gold; nine packs of chewing gum; one issue of prophylactics; three lipsticks; and three pairs of nylon stockings. Shoot, a fella' could have a pretty good weekend in Vegas with all that stuff.'

– Major "King" Kong in *Dr. Strangelove*

Strangelove is surely also deeply psychological. One critic summed up the film by saying that the dark elements provide its most meaningful moments. 'They are made up of the incongruities, the banalities, and the misunderstandings that we are constantly aware of in our lives. On the brink of annihilation, they become irresistibly absurd.'[147]

Strangelove illustrates very well a theory called 'benign violation,' an idea presented to a wider audience by Giovanni Sabato in an article for *The*

---

[147] FilmReference.com

Scientific American called 'What's So Funny? The Science of Why We Laugh[148].' Sabato starts by recalling that for more than 2,000 years, pundits have assumed that all forms of humor share a common ingredient. The oldest theory, Sabato says, dates back to the ancient Greeks and is that it favors the idea that people find humor in and laugh at earlier versions of themselves and the misfortunes of others because of feeling superior. Then there's the theory of release, best known in the form presented by Freud, which I would say fits *Strangelove* very well too. With the punch line comes a pleasurable "release" of energy, such as laughter, that had been up until then needed to suppress anxiety or socially disprove emotions such as lust and hostility.

And in dark humor, there's another long-standing aspect, the one highlighted by Immanuel Kant, Arthur Schopenhauer, and Henri Bergson (and others), which is the vital ingredient of incongruity.

Recall perhaps the joke that opens with Woody Allen's film *Annie Hall*. Allen describes the case of two elderly women seen at a holiday resort, one of whom says, 'Boy, the food at this place is really terrible.' The other one replies, 'Yeah, I know, and such small portions.' Allen goes on to quip: "Well, that's essentially how I feel about life—full of loneliness, misery, suffering, unhappiness, and it's all over much too quickly."

People laugh at the juxtaposition of incompatible concepts and at the defiance of their expectations—that is, at the incongruity between expectations and reality. Here, the "dark" aspect is this overturning of the reassuring framework of logic and commonsense.

However, Giovanni Sabato says of the three main theories that, although they certainly capture something about what makes us laugh, they are insufficient. It is this perceived gap that led Peter McGraw and Caleb Warren, professors both at the University of Colorado Boulder, to propose a new theory of "benign violation" in order, they said, both to unify the previous research and to address its limits. Benign violation derives from the theory of incongruity, but it goes deeper by proposing that humor results when we simultaneously recognize that an ethical, social, or physical norm (I would add "logical" to the list, too) has been violated, as well as that this violation is not *very* offensive or upsetting. Things such as time, geography, and social distance can reduce the sense of offense.

---

[148] *Scientific American* 2019

Yet how can all these very different, indeed in some ways opposed, functions of humor—promoting social bonding or excluding others with derision—be reconciled?

One way to unify the different aspects of humor is to look at it as a biologist might and seek to explain it in terms of evolutionary processes. David Sloan Wilson and Matthew Gervais, for example, have tried to shed light on the workings of humor by distinguishing two different kinds of laughter. Spontaneous, emotional, impulsive, and involuntary laughter, they say, is a genuine expression of amusement and joy that comes as part of playing; it shows up in the smiles of a child or during roughhousing or tickling. Such displays of amusement (also identified by Freud) have a name called *Duchenne* laughter, after Guillaume-Benjamin-Amand Duchenne de Boulogne, who described it in the mid-19th century. Conversely, "non-Duchenne" laughter is contrived imitation. It is the polite chuckle offered as a social strategy—for example, to punctuate ordinary conversations, even those that are not particularly funny. To that point, though.

According to Wilson and Gervais, spontaneous laughter has its roots in the games of early primates, while controlled laughter evolved later, along with the development of casual conversation, denigration, and derision in social interactions.

Naturally, being biologists, they also try to explain things in terms of bodily parts, and so the authors say of Duchenne laughter that it arises in the brain stem and the limbic system (responsible for emotions), whereas non-Duchenne laughter is controlled by what they call the voluntary premotor areas (thought to participate in planning movements) of the frontal cortex. The neural mechanisms are so distinct that just one pathway or the other is affected by some forms of facial paralysis. What is of more interest to us here, though, is their idea that laughter evolved as a group response to what Wilson and Gervais call *protohumor*—non-serious violations of social norms. The humor and the laughter were reliable indicators of relaxed, safe times.[149]

Of course, other biologists offer other, simpler accounts of humor's role in evolution, for example, the dating ads "GSOH essential" idea that humor and laughter play a part in the selection of sexual partners, or the again, rather

---

[149] Wilson and Gervais 2005

literal notion that jokes and laughter have a socially useful role in the damping of aggression and conflict.

A rather different suggestion for an evolutionary function of humor is that laughter is a public sign of our ability to recognize discrepancies. It elevates our social status and allows us to attract reproductive partners. And because grasping the incongruities requires a store of knowledge and beliefs, shared laughter signals a commonality of worldviews, preferences, and convictions, which reinforces social ties and the sense of belonging to the same group.

The approach appears in a recent book by Matthew Hurley, Daniel Dennett, and Reginald Adams, called *Inside Jokes: Using Humor to Reverse-Engineer the Mind*, which also seeks an "evolutionary advantage" for joking around. Their grandly named 'evolutionary/neuro-computational' model is premised on the idea that "every emotion begets a set of behaviors that generate a lasting, durable advantage"...some 'substantially important cognitive task'[150]. With a nod, in passing at the American comedian Lily Tomlin's sardonic claim that Man first walked upright to free his hands for masturbation, they say that if we are to understand our "addiction" to laughter, we need to recognize that:

'Humor is always related to some kind of mistake. Every pun, joke, and comic incident seems to contain a fool of some sort—the "butt" of the joke.'

Ah-ha! Yet this insight immediately obliges them to ask, 'Why do we enjoy mistakes?' and so to propose that it is not the mistakes *per se* that people enjoy; it is the emotional reward for discovering and thus undoing mistakes in thought.

Actually, dark humor does seem to involve a lot of mistakes and misfortune generally, but in this sweeping account, which attempts to unify not only 'word play,' the 'rubber-faced antics' of comedians and even musical jokes, dark humor itself gets little attention other than a literal (I suppose that they would say 'logical') observation that navy pilots use dark humor to cope with the fearful aspects of dangerous take-offs and landings on aircraft carriers. Or, as they put it, 'Joking about the disastrous—using the negatively valanced content to create a positively valanced emotion—gives them the necessary levity to perform their difficult job.'[151] Incidentally, if you're not sure what

---

[150] Hurley et al, pages 76 and 54
[151] Hurley et al, 285

"valanced" means here, abstracted from its original context in chemistry, neither have I. (It's such an odd term that even my spellchecker hates it.)

Of course, other researchers have also linked jokes to high-stress work[152]. It has been claimed that gallows humor plays a large role in a firefighter's ability to manage and overcome trauma. One wrote that:

'Having witnessed the interactions of firefighters in day rooms, humor is intertwined into almost all conversations. There is more banter, friendly interrogations, sarcastic comments, and jokes involving everyone, and their mother heard between firefighters than in almost any other workplace I have stepped foot in.'[153]

A paper in the *Journal of Holistic Nursing Practice*[154] suggests that medical staff should increase their beneficial laughter by exposing themselves to humorous material or undertaking humor training.

However, responding to similar proposals that ambulance staff should be taught how to tell jokes to help them cope with unpleasant situations, researcher Sarah Christopher has doubts about the 'one size fits all' approach to wit, writing plainly, 'This is an extremely doubtful strategy when considering black humor. Firstly, humor is ephemeral by nature and a very personal thing. What appears funny to one person may not appear so to another. Secondly, the events and situations faced by emergency services personnel can in no way be perceived as objectively funny in themselves, particularly to those who have not been exposed to the role.'[155] She adds that research suggests that spontaneity is the primary requirement for therapeutic humor, as opposed to being a conscious attempt at coping.

Support for the idea that people should be trained to find upsetting things funny comes from a study into the dark side of humor. Herzog and Karafa (1998) looked at whether the preference for sick jokes, a category classified as 'death, death-baby, general and handicapped,' as compared to non-sick jokes, categorized as 'nonsense, social satire, philosophical, sexual hostile, demeaning to men and women, ethnic and scatological jokes.'

The authors note that earlier studies (somewhat in the timeless tradition of dog bites man reports) discerned a positive correlation between "aggressive

---

[152] Kobassa and Puccetti 1983, Rosenberg 1981

[153] Alvarado, G. 2013, Moran C 1990

[154] Wooten 1996

[155] Christopher 2015

mood" and the enjoyment of aggressive humor, and so it might have been expected that their study would find that "subjects who enjoy reading cartoons dealing with nasty or morbid contents also show high levels of aggression". However, they found quite the contrary! Aggressive people seemed to not appreciate or even understand the jokes of black humor. This linked up with earlier findings that people who found "sick" jokes amusing had the ability to treat nasty contents as playful fiction.

In other words, as films like *Doctor Strangelove* illustrate very well, it does seem that liking nasty jokes does not mean you are nasty. Better! As the *Cognitive Studies* contributors, Willinger *et al.*, think, 'a strong association between black humor processing and verbal as well as non-verbal intellectual capacities can be shown.' This may not be entirely surprising. If a joke relies on the detection of incongruities, then it also relies on a degree of intelligence and contextual knowledge. Such research fits with Freud's assertion that subjects with high socio-economic status are more appreciative of aggressive humor, as long as it is thought to be within the bounds of "good taste", a reference point that is clearly rather wobbly.

Take the topic of the Holocaust. The idea of humor in the Holocaust may, to many, be an offensive concept. And yet, as a Holocaust survivor consulted in a study[156] said, 'When I was interviewed for Spielberg and they asked me what I thought was the reason I survived, they probably expected me to answer good fortune or other things. I said that I thought it was laughter or humor.' Likewise, Emil Fackenheim, philosopher and Auschwitz survivor, says simply: 'We kept our morale through humor'[157]. It looks more like Sarah Christopher says: 'Black humor cannot be described as being pessimistic or simply lacking an affirmative moral voice. Rather, it lives outside these limits in a terrain of terrifying candor concerning the most extreme situations.'[158]

For Freud anyway, dark humor, by being aggressive, is nasty and deplorable.

'By belittling and humbling our enemy, by scorning and ridiculing him, we indirectly obtain the pleasure of his defeat by the laughter of the third person, the inactive spectator. We are now prepared for the role that wit plays in hostile aggression. Wit permits us to make our enemy ridiculous through

---

[156] Ostrower 1998

[157] Feig 1979

[158] Christopher 2015

that which we could not utter loudly or consciously on account of existing hindrances; in other words, wit affords us the means of surmounting restrictions and of opening up otherwise inaccessible pleasure sources. were wont to overestimate the substance of the sentence wittily expressed.'[159]

Freud offers the following, quite lengthy, example of aggression being clothed as wit.

One Wendell Phillips was lecturing in Ohio, and while on a railroad journey, he met a number of clergymen returning from some sort of convention. One of the ministers, feeling called upon to approach Mr. Phillips, asked him, 'Are you Mr. Phillips?'

'I am, sir.'

'Are you trying to free the niggers?'

'Yes, sir; I am an abolitionist.'

'Well, why do you preach your doctrines up here? Why don't you go over into Kentucky?'

'Excuse me, are you a preacher?' *

'I am, sir.'

'Are you trying to save souls from hell?'

'Yes, sir, that's my business.'

'Well, why don't you go there?'

The assailant hurried into the smoker amid a roar of unsanctified laughter. This anecdote nicely illustrates the tendency to use wit in the service of hostile aggression. The minister's behavior was offensive and irritating, yet Wendell Phillips, as a man of culture, could not defend himself in the same manner as a common, ill-bred person would have done and as his inner feelings must have prompted him to do. The only alternative under the circumstances would have been to take the affront in silence, had not wit shown him the way, and enabled him by the technical means of unification to turn the tables on his assailant. He not only belittled him and turned him into ridicule, but by his clever retort, 'Well, why don't you go there?' fascinated the other clergymen, and thus brought them to his side.'

As I say, humor research depends rather on the researcher's own sense of humor. And Freud himself does not seem very interested in aggressive wit. Indeed, he even wrote:

---

[159] Freud 1922, 151-2

'For our theoretical explanation of the nature of wit, harmless wit must be of greater value to us than tendency wit and shallow wit more than profound wit. Harmless and shallow plays on words present to us the problem of wit in its purest form, because of the good sense therein and because there is no purposive factor nor an underlying philosophy to confuse the judgment. With such material, our understanding can make further progress.'[160]

Freud seems early on to have defined wit as, in principle, a fine thing: He writes: 'The technical means of wit which we have described, such as condensation, displacement, indirect expression, etc., have therefore the faculty to produce a feeling of pleasure in the hearer,' And he goes on it is 'the laughableness (*Lacheffekt*) that constitutes the pleasure of wit.'[161]

But not so with aggressive wit. Here, Freud says, we laugh despite ourselves; we often feel we ought not to laugh! This ambiguous response is, of course, at the heart of dark humor.

Herzog and Karafa (1998) looked at whether the preference for sick jokes, a category classified as 'death, death-baby, general, and handicapped,' as compared to non-sick jokes, was categorized as 'nonsense, social satire, philosophical, sexual hostility, demeaning to men and women, ethnic, and scatological jokes.'

The authors note that earlier studies (somewhat in the timeless tradition of dog bites man reports) discerned a positive correlation between "aggressive mood" and the enjoyment of aggressive humor, and so it might have been expected that their study would find that 'subjects who enjoy reading cartoons dealing with nasty or morbid contents also show high levels of aggression.' However, they found quite the contrary! Aggressive people seemed to not appreciate or even understand the jokes of black humor. This linked up with earlier findings that people who found "sick" jokes amusing had the ability to treat nasty contents as playful fiction.

In other words, as films like *Doctor Strangelove* illustrate very well, it does seem that liking nasty jokes does not mean you are nasty. Better! As the *Cognitive Studies* contributors, Willinger *et al.*, think, 'a strong association between black humor processing and verbal as well as non-verbal intellectual capacities can be shown.' This may not be entirely surprising. If a joke relies on the detection of incongruities, then it also relies on a degree of intelligence

---

[160] Freud 1922, 134
[161] Freud 1922, 135

and contextual knowledge. Such research fits with Freud's assertion that subjects with high socio-economic status are more appreciative of aggressive humor, as long as it is thought to be within the bounds of "good taste", a reference point that is clearly rather wobbly.

As I say, humor research depends rather on the researcher's own sense of humor. And Freud himself does not seem very interested in aggressive wit. Indeed, he even writes:

'For our theoretical explanation of the nature of wit, harmless wit must be of greater value to us than tendency wit and shallow wit more than profound wit. Harmless and shallow plays on words present to us the problem of wit in its purest form, because of the good sense therein and because there is no purposive factor nor an underlying philosophy to confuse the judgment. With such material, our understanding can make further progress.'[162]

Freud seems early on to have defined wit as, in principle, a fine thing: He writes: 'The technical means of wit which we have described, such as condensation, displacement, indirect expression, etc., have therefore the faculty to produce a feeling of pleasure in the hearer,' And he goes on, 'the laughableness (*Lacheffekt*) that constitutes the pleasure of wit.'

But not so with aggressive wit. Here, Freud says, we laugh despite ourselves; we often feel we ought not to laugh! This ambiguous response is, of course, at the heart of dark humor.

Nonetheless, Freud does see it as having a positive role. "The first use of wit, which goes beyond the mere production of pleasure, points out the road to be followed. Wit is now recognized as a powerful psychic factor whose weight can determine the issue if it falls on this or that side of the scale. The great tendencies and impulses of our psychic life enlist its service for their own purposes. The original purposeless wit, which began as play, becomes related in a secondary manner to tendencies from which nothing that is formed in psychic life can escape for any length of time."

Freud seemed to sum up the essence of dark humor all those years ago when he wrote:

'It begins as play in order to obtain pleasure from the free use of words and thoughts. As soon as the growing reason forbids this senseless play with words and thoughts, it turns to the jest or joke in order to hold on to these sources of

---

[162] Freud 1922, 134

pleasure and to be able to gain new pleasure from the liberation of the absurd. In the role of harmless wit, it assists the thoughts and fortifies them against the impugnment of the critical judgment, whereby it makes use of the principle of intermingling the pleasure sources. Finally, it enters into the great struggle of suppressed tendencies in order to remove inner inhibitions in accordance with the principle of fore-pleasure. Reason, critical judgment, and suppression—these are the forces that it combats in turn.'[163]

More recently, a study published in the journal *Cognitive Process*, citing numerous sources, says that people who like humor that is on the darker side have higher IQs. Ulrike Willinger *et al.* pronounce that wit is a complex information-processing task, 'relying heavily on intellectual as well as other cognitive abilities.'

The researchers reason that dark humor requires more brainpower to process how the jokes work compared to more standard gags. In particular, they highlight a feature they named 'frame blending.' This is where the premise of a joke is set up, or "framed," in one way and then shifted into a different frame for comedic effect. They accept that most humor is built this way—the incongruity of an unexpected twist in a joke leads to laughs. But they think that the "frame blending" of dark humor requires an extra step and more cognitive resources since the conscious mind would have to overcome its distaste for the inappropriate subject matter in order to get to the punchline of the joke.

To prove it, Willinger *et al.* devised an experiment to demonstrate this that involved showing twelve "bleak and satirical" cartoons by the German cartoonist Uli Stein to participants whose intelligence had been previously assessed by means of standard IQ tests. We might wonder how funny the cartoons were, given that the experiment required the participants to rate their comprehension and their enjoyment of each one.

Uli is best known for his anthropomorphic animals, like the grumpy dog who is being taught how to balance a dog biscuit on his nose by his owner and is thinking, 'That's it. I'm going to kill him.' But these are not cartoons like that. Instead, for example, one of the images showed two people at a morgue, one of whom was a man in a lab coat lifting a sheet covering a body. The

---

[163] Freud 1922, 211

woman standing next to him confirms: 'Sure, that's my husband. Anyway, which washing powder did you use to get that so white?'[164]

I don't myself find this joke very funny, which reminds me that the problem, as ever, with humor research is that what the researchers use as examples of something funny…is not necessarily funny. We would hesitate to test the chemical composition of granite with random pieces of rock from the garden, but with "funny jokes" that seems to be pretty much the system.

But methodology be damned (for a moment), the *Cognitive Processing* study found that those who appreciated and understood the jokes received high verbal and non-verbal IQ test results, were better educated and scored lower for aggression and bad mood. On the face of it, we would all be better off practicing laughing at jokes rather than risking being considered stupid and grumpy. And yet, the problem remains. What if not all jokes and not all cartoons are funny? Because if you use unfunny ones in a test, you risk the result that the test will score highly on people who do not have a sense of humor.

I think we all know, from our everyday interactions, the problem of unfunny jokes. Dark humor, for obvious reasons, must tread the line precariously.

However, Giovannantonio Forabosco, a psychologist and editor of an Italian journal devoted to studies of humor, pushes back against any such simple distinctions. He rejects the very idea of "one size fits all" approaches, saying, 'It is presumptuous to think about cracking the secret of humor with a unified theory.' And he goes on:

'We understand many aspects of it, and now the neurosciences are helping to clarify important issues. But as for its essence, it's like saying, "Let's define the essence of love." We can study it from many different angles; we can measure the effect of the sight of the beloved on a lover's heart rate. But that doesn't explain love. It's the same with humor. In fact, I always refer to it by describing it, never by defining it.'[165]

And directly addressing something that many theorists, from Freud on, seem to have shied away from, Forabosco thinks that elements like aggression, sexuality, sadism, and cynicism add punch to a joke. 'They don't have to be there, but the funniest jokes are those in which they are.'

---

[164] Willinger *et al*

[165] *Scientific American* June 26 2019

Freud distinguishes between "harmless wit" and "tendency wit", which, by implication, is not harmless.

Today's analysts of wit, however, have a much more positive view of dark humor. As the amusingly named Conrad Knickerbocker wrote in the *New York Times:*

'By default, the black humorists have become keepers of conscience. Strident, apt, they challenge the hypnotists and the hysterics. They urge choices on us. Amid the banality, the emptiness, and excess, they offer the terrors and possibilities of self-knowledge.'[166]

---

[166] *New York Times*, 1964

Chapter 12
Animals Being Funny

Birds are great mimics, a skill that sometimes crosses over into mischief-making for fun. Pictured is a humble sparrow. Engraving by P. Tempest, ca. 1690, after F. Barlo
(The Welcome Library, London.)

I'm not sure how many people have a sense of humor. Or, to be precise, given they invariably *think* they do have one, it's not a good fit with mine. But put all that to one side for a moment and ask: Do *animals* have a sense of humor? At the start of this book, I mentioned that, as long ago as the nineteenth century, this question was being seriously discussed among scholars. Charles Darwin, in particular, described chimpanzees giggling as they played. He wrote:

'The imagination is sometimes said to be tickled by a ludicrous idea, and this so-called tickling of the mind is curiously analogous with that of the body. Everyone knows how immoderately children laugh and how their whole bodies are convulsed when they are tickled. The anthropoid apes, as we have seen, likewise utter a reiterated sound, corresponding with our laughter, when they are tickled, especially under the armpits.'

This was in a little-known essay called 'On the Expression of Emotions in Man and Animals.' Here, Darwin went on to allow animals to enjoy a joke in a superficial, physical sense. And indeed, anyone who has played with a dog will have had the very clear impression that the animal is both enjoying the game and also (more subtly) participating in it. When a dog fetches a stick and drops it to be thrown, the dog seems to be performing an act that surely, in practical terms, is counterproductive (the dog wants the stick) but can be understood in emotional terms—the dog wants the fun of chasing the stick again.

Recall again here Charles Darwin's observations on dogs and sticks, made as part of his examination of similarities in emotions between animals and humans in *The Descent of Man*. He describes one of the species' favorite jokes there.

Animal Joke #1

'Dogs show what may be fairly called a sense of humor, as distinct from mere play; if a bit of stick…is thrown to one, he will often carry it away for a short distance, and then, squatting down with it on the ground close before him, he will wait until his master comes quite close to take it away. The dog will then seize it and rush away in triumph, repeating the same maneuver and evidently enjoying the practical joke.'

However, Darwin misses one detail. The ethnologist Konrad Lorenz would later observe in his book *Man Meets Dog,* of which more later, that the panting noise dogs make in fetching sticks is actually them laughing. Additional research conducted by Patricia Simonet, an animal behaviorist at the Spokane Animal Shelter in Washington, followed this up by looking specifically at the laughing sounds in dogs. Simonet's team investigated the question by standing in parks with a parabolic microphone that allowed them to record the sounds that dogs made while playing from a distance.

Simonet found that dogs actually have a very specific "pant" when they play. Using a spectrograph, they analyzed the sound and identified a distinctive 'pronounced breathy forced exhalation.' The significance of the sound was underlined by playing it with other dogs. When they heard it, the dogs responded by play-bowing, wagging their tails, or play-chasing. So, what does a dog laughing sound like? Simonet says that, 'To an untrained human ear, it sounds much like a pant, *hhuh, hhuh*.' Or, maybe, dogs are a bit "French" and don't pronounce their aitches. Thus, "Ha Ha Ha" becomes "Ah-Ah-Ah"!

Well, that makes sense, we might say skeptically. Yet we should not be too dismissive. Nancy Hill, Simonet's boss at the shelter, was originally doubtful of the approach too. As she told ABC News:

'I thought: Laughing dogs? A sound that we're gonna isolate and play in the shelter? I was a real skeptic...until we played the recording here at the shelter.'

Because when they played the sound of a dog panting in the ordinary sense over the loudspeaker, the gaggle of dogs at the shelter kept right on barking. But when they played the dog version of laughing, all fifteen barking dogs went quiet within about a minute.

'It was a night-and-day difference,' Hill said. 'It was absolutely phenomenal.'[167]

So research seems to convincingly show that dogs laugh. But what is both more demanding and more interesting to ask is, can animals tell jokes? This is what we will investigate in this, the final chapter of the book.

Researchers at the Gorilla Foundation, a wonderful organization dedicated to the preservation, protection, and well-being of gorillas and other great apes, say that they can. The Foundation reports, for example, that Koko, a gorilla in Woodside, California, who learned more than 2,000 words and 1,000 American Sign Language signs, had the most subtle of humor skills—the ability to play with different meanings of the same word. When once she was asked, 'What can you think of that's hard?' the gorilla signed, "rock" and 'work.' Another time, she tied her trainer's shoelaces together and signed, 'chase.'

The Foundation also claims that since Koko understood English as well as sign language, she often had fun with sounds. In an article entitled 'Gorillas just wanna have fun,' Gary Stanley, the Chief Operating Officer of the Foundation, recalled that Koko enjoyed all kinds of rhyming poetry and even made plays on words, such as when one time she put a straw to her nose and signed herself as a "thirsty elephant". Likewise, on another occasion, she combined her own name, "Koko" and "nut" to make "coconut".[168]

---

[167] **Chapter 12** ABC News 2005
[168] Koko.org 2010

But do animals display such "humor behavior" to get reactions from others—or just for their own pleasure? Some researchers think they do have a sense of the audience. Several anecdotes shared on the internet forum of the Animal Welfare Institute attribute just such humorous intent. One (unnamed) participant wrote:

Animal Joke #2

'My most memorable experience was a while back when I worked with young chimpanzees…One female in particular would often take a blanket and put it over her head, like a little ghost. She would then chase the other chimps around. They would run away, screaming and smiling. The little "ghost" would then suddenly pull that blanket off, and the other chimps would laugh and laugh. It looked like a human game of tag, and they definitely seemed to enjoy it.'[169]

Another story mentioned on the site concerns the British zoologist Miriam Rothschild's parrot, who apparently would call her dog's name and whistle. When the dog dutifully went up to the parrot's cage, the parrot laughed at it. This underlined, the participant said, the fact that parrots regularly figure in stories of animals 'causing trouble to get a reaction' and the participant went on to give another example.

Animal Joke #3

'Many years ago, when I managed a pet store, I had a scarlet macaw that would wait until I had swept the floor. Then he would proceed to take his beak, scoop the seed out of his bowl, and fling it across the floor. When the bowl was empty, he would stick his head upside down in it and laugh as loud as he could (he liked the echo of the bowl) until I swept it all up.'[170]

It has often been observed that many animals will "laugh" as a reaction to certain social situations that are pleasing to them. Another way to put it is that they show themselves to be able to communicate their emotional state. This kind of communication seems to be there in the wagging of a dog's tail, which

---

[169] AWI 2011
[170] AWI 2011

is also, of course, closely linked to play and any kind of social interaction. More dramatic and rather extraordinary, though, is the element of emotional communication revealed in the paintings of animals. The art of apes, bonobos, and chimpanzees has been much noted, but slightly less so for paintings of humbler animals like horses, pigs, dolphins, and elephants. Yet all these animals have proven themselves to be genuinely creative with the paintbrush.

In an article for the journal, now web magazine, *The Philosopher* (the real one, the one founded in 1923 as well as the one which I've edited for donkey's years), John Valentine recalls what the biologist, Desmond Morris, formulated in his book, *The Biology of Art*, as an approach to understanding these intriguing examples of 'animal artists.' Morris explains that Congo, the most prolific chimpanzee painter at the London Zoo, consistently demonstrated seven distinctive patterns of behavior during various drawing and painting experiments.

1. An intense focus on the blank sheets of paper presented to him and the markings he produced.
2. An aversion to being interrupted while drawing or painting.
3. Careful restriction of mark-making to the blank paper itself.
4. Periodically marking blank paper with a fan pattern that underwent numerous repetitions over time.
5. Balancing offset figures. For example, a square figure presented to him just to the right of the center on the paper was balanced by mark-making an equal distance to the left of the center.
6. A quantifiable progression in the styles of his compositional and calligraphic skills. (Although Congo never reached the representational stage, he went through numerous scribbling and diagrammatic stages that seem to be precursors to representational drawing and that are found in human children.)
7. And above all, finding his drawing or painting to be a rewarding activity in itself without any connection to outside positive reinforcement.

An eighth indication that Congo really was doing "art" was that he seemed to treat painting as a special kind of activity that held a different value for him than regular play or roughhousing.

And finally, Valentine notes, Congo reliably demonstrated resistance to any direct positive reinforcement that was used to make him paint.

"In this last sense, Congo was similar to another chimpanzee who was once subjected to bribery with a food reward to encourage him to draw more intensely. He quickly learned to associate drawing with getting the reward, but as soon as this condition was established, he took less and less interest in the lines he was drawing. As Morris notes, 'Any old scribble would do', and then he would immediately hold out his hand for the reward. The careful attention he had paid previously to design, rhythm, balance, and composition was gone, and the worst kind of commercial art was born!"[171]

Such accounts should make us rethink our attitudes toward animals and their abilities. But although gorillas, of course, are our human cousins, it is *dogs* that are our human companions, and so, for many reasons, it is dogs that we tend to feel we share certain feelings with, even if, admittedly, dogs are rather poor painters. It is dogs who we find easiest to imagine sharing a joke with us. Other animals, however, seem very different, and yet they too have been observed to enjoy the occasional witticism. Take rats, for example. In an article for the website 'Exploring Your Mind,' it is pointed out that:

'Rats have been around humans for a long time. However, the stigma attached to them has meant that almost no one has taken an interest in their emotionality or their social relationships. For those who love these rodents, the difficulty is that most of the sounds they make aren't audible to humans.'[172]

However, contrary to the website, back in 1998, there was a study in the *Journal of Comparative Psychology* that did shed a little more light on the hitherto unsuspected world of rat play. The rats were found to be emitting "laughter" sounds in social playing situations, or at least, 'short, high-frequency ultrasonic vocalizations' at approximately 50 kHz. Furthermore, the rats "laughed" more, depending on whether they could see other rats and whether they associated the chamber they were in with previous games.[173]

Expanding the scope of such research to take a closer look at the phenomenon of laughter across the animal kingdom, primatologist and UCLA anthropology graduate student Sasha Winkler and UCLA professor of communication Greg Bryant found examples of vocal play behavior

---

[171] Valentine 2012

[172] exploringyourmind.com 2021

[173] Knutson et al 1998

documented in at least sixty-five species. Their list includes not only a variety of the usual primates and domestic dogs, but also foxes, seals, cows, and mongooses, as well as several types of birds, including parakeets and Australian magpies.

To create their list, the UCLA pair combed through the existing scientific literature on animal play behavior, looking for mentions of vocal play signals—or what might be thought of as the equivalent of human laughter.[174] A shortcut used by many studies to produce this "laughter" involves the tickling of animals. As Darwin noted, chimpanzees, bonobos, gorillas, and orangutans all produce laughter-like sounds when tickled, but so do many more animals, at least if you know where to tickle them. However, the kinds of explanations traditionally offered for human laughter, such as that it derives from a sense of superiority or alternatively, a sense of conceptual confusion, seem a stretch to apply to humble tickling, whether for animals or humans.

Which is why, in recent years, psychologists have come up with a different theory. The new idea was that laughter is sometimes a response to a situation where something happens that both seems to threaten either a person's or an animal's autonomy while also being perceived as essentially "okay" and non-threatening. This theory is dubbed "Benign Violation". It seems to explain why a number of things that make us laugh, including being tickled, work across the human-animal divide.

"Benign Violation" also explains behavior in terms of an individual and their immediate environment. But a rather different insight into what may lie behind both animal and human laughter is the idea that our perhaps rather significantly termed "sense of humor" is an evolutionary necessity for any animal that lives in a social group. Evidence offered for this comes from wolves, who are doubly interesting as they are, of course, the ancestors of today's dogs, and yet they still live in hierarchal packs where it's essential for each animal to know its place and avoid angering the alpha wolf. And laughter, for wolves, seems to be a form of submissive behavior.

Which puts another aspect to the well-noted phenomenon of "nervous laughter", say when someone is being picked upon and humiliated. Think: Your dog comes when called; you give it a dog treat. She fetches the stick, and she gets rewarded. She rolls her back on the floor with a goofy expression, and

---

[174] Winkler & Bryant 2021

her tummy tickles. All in all, it seems possible that dogs, more than any other animals, display elements of what we think of as a sense of humor to get a response. The joke is on us!

But this is a rather meager tribute to the playful nature of man's best friend. In the book mentioned above, Konrad Lorenz suggests dogs not only understand human laughter, they have their own ways of laughing too. He writes:

'...the slightly opened jaws, which reveal the tongue, and the tilted angle of the mouth, which stretches almost from ear to ear, give a still stronger impression of laughter, which makes them so excited that they soon start panting.'[175]

Lorenz's dog, laughing, by the way, is described as having huffing, breathy "laugh pant" behavior.

Lorenz's book, which also contains some appallingly racist comments about aboriginals, people he describes as "of extraordinarily low cultural standing" and even calls the 'non-marsupial mammals of Australia,' reminds us of two things. First, humans often assume animals are stupid just because they do not understand the way animals think, and secondly, humans also ascribe similar stupidity to other people for exactly the same failure of imagination. In sharp contrast, Bruce Chatwin's book, *Songlines*, powerfully communicates the extraordinary, ancient, and subtle culture of the Australian Aborigines. Yet Lorenz, who is so empathetic and aware of animal behavior, is evidently a poor judge of his fellow humans. Nonetheless, another thing Lorenz asks is well worth thinking about, and this is how often we have seen animals playing jokes—either on us or on other animals—only maybe not quite realized it. He describes, for example, the behavior of a lemur called Maxi, who was regularly and aggressively chased by his dogs. Lorenz again:

'This, however, only seemed to amuse her, nor were they entirely to blame, for Maxi's favorite joke was to steal up from behind, tweak one of the dogs in the rump or pull its tail, and then swing herself up into a tree, where, from a safe height, she dangled her tail just out of reach of the infuriated dogs.'[176]

I've suggested that we tend to underestimate the thinking that goes on behind the behavior of animals, but the reverse error is true of our pets. An owner will often ascribe very complex reasoning and behavior strategies to

---

[175] Lorenz 2002, 58
[176] Lorenz 2002, 101

their own dog or cat, but not to dogs and cats. Generally, Lorenz offers that this difference in perception is not as unscientific as it might seem. He writes:

'Nobody can assess the mental qualities of a dog without having once possessed the love of one, and the same thing applies to many other intelligent socially living animals, such as ravens, jackdaws, large parrots, wild geese and monkeys.' [177]

What, though, about cats, conspicuously missing from the list? 'The mind of the cat is a delicate and wild thing, not easily disclosed to the type of person who forces his love obtrusively on an animal,' writes Lorenz. And how much more difficult is it to say if they share a sense of fun with humans?

Writing in the *New York Times* some forty years ago, James Gorman offended many cat lovers by answering in the negative. One reader wrote in (this was back in the days of actual letters) to say he would like to see Gorman eaten by a Doberman, while another suggested he should be in a mental hospital. Ho ho ho! But after twenty or so years of reflection, Gorman wrote a new piece announcing that, in any case, he had had second thoughts on cats and their elusive sense of humor.

Where he had earlier argued that dogs were, in evolutionary terms, animals using laughter to facilitate life in the pack and that the dogs with the laughter gene survived and the ones without it didn't, he now thought that laughter can serve different, meaning more, purposes. Specifically, it can be friendly or submissive, hostile or dominant. He recalled the old distinction between laughing *with* and laughing *at* someone. Perhaps, the thing he had missed about cats was that yes, they don't seem to laugh with their owners so much—the famous haughty cat—but maybe they did have a sense of humor, only it emerged mostly with them laughing *at* their owner!

'With a mouse, or a ball of yarn, a cat may play and be amused, whether we are watching or not.' And Gorman offered an olive branch to his cat-lover owners:

'So, I'm now prepared to acknowledge that some cats may have a sense of humor. It's very dry and slightly wicked, I'll bet.'

Okay, let's allow that at least some animals, just as we allow that at least some humans, have a sense of humor. But more than that, can this comparison with animals give us a particular insight into this very special kind of behavior?

---

[177] Lorenz 2002, 158

Over the course of this book, we've considered three general theories as to the function of jokes and wit generally. There's Plato's claim that it is about feelings of superiority; there's Henri Bergson and Arthur Schopenhauer's idea that it's all about pleasure in observing incongruity; and finally there's the new idea that it is about 'benign violation.' Making mischief, in other words. There are also a raft of other theories that I've not been inclined to mention. But now, at the end of the investigation, the fact is that *all* the theories seem to offer a bit of the truth about jokes and humor, with the aspect that is surely most distinctively human being the pleasure obtained from the contradictory, the absurd, and the ridiculous. It's a naughty pleasure largely drummed out of us in everyday life. But maybe we should begin to value it a bit more.

Afterword
Let the Fun Begin!

So, enough theory; now let's get practical. How to be funny? In a moment, I'll try to pull together the threads in this book—the philosophers' views, the sociologists' insights—and give you some practical tips to take away and ramp up being "funny" with. I'll share the insights of author and compere on the UK comedy circuit, Dominic Frisby, who has a very particular view that curiously echoes that of the philosophers. But, to start us off, here is Kendall Payne, a writer, director, and stand-up comedian based in Brooklyn, New York, who has kindly agreed to share her expert view, well, not with me personally, but with the whole world via an online guide (Wikihow, 31 August 2022). This has three parts prefaced by the big question of 'How to be Funny,' before going on to 'Developing a Sense of Humor,' 'Developing a Funny Personality,' and last but not least, 'Staying Inspired.'

First of all, and remember, Kendall does stand-up, so she must know a bit about it. She says that being naturally funny is actually a skill you can practice and get better at. She suggests, optimistically, that by exploring your sense of humor and playing around with it in different situations, you'll be surprised at how quickly being funny becomes second nature. Work out what kind of joker you are: some of us enjoy sarcastic and witty comments (or maybe so-called "ironic comedy" where the meaning of the joke is the opposite of the actual meaning), others are suckers for wordplay, some like impressions, and others still enjoy funny actions. Some of us are good at telling stories—anecdotal comedy—which may or may not be embellished; some of us have a very dry humor delivered with no expression or matter of fact, while by contrast, others are amusing precisely because of the drama and exaggeration. (So-called hyperbolic comedy)

All of these are legitimate strategies to choose from in the quest to be funny, but it is best to pick something that genuinely fits your personality. Better a bad joke of your own than a good joke that is obviously borrowed. Countervailing, several other sections of the advice are to 'broaden your knowledge of funny material,' 'Read, read, read. Get your hands on anything and everything that is funny and consume it like your mom told you not to…' 'Read joke books. It won't hurt to have a few good jokes memorized' and yes, 'Memorize some one-liners' because:

'One-liners can steal the show. Dorothy Parker was brilliant with one-liners; for example, when told that Calvin Coolidge had died, she replied, "How can they tell?"'[178]

So it seems that there's a bit of tension between the need to be original and the advantages of learning from others. We're advised to 'Avoid memorizing and re-telling older jokes.' (Bang goes my last remaining strategy for being funny!)

But actually, Kendall mainly warns against appearing 'unnatural and rehearsed.' Another contemporary stand-up, Dominic Frisby, as we'll see in a moment, emphasizes the importance of knowing your "material", and briskly rejects the idea that comics rely on spontaneous wit. But both Kendall and Frisby agree that the jokes have to be delivered as if apparently conjured up by the moment. Put another way, the art of being funny is much less about being original than it is about technique. As the old adage has it, it's not what you say, it's how you tell 'em.

Another point Kendall stresses, related to 'Being Funny in a Social Situation,' is to connect with your audience. This is really crucial. Humor just is social. Kendall says to pitch your humor so as not to offend, and that means to tone it down for the old folks, no joking about religion or politics, no making fun of people's appearance or beliefs, and hey! Kendall just became really boring.

On the other hand, Kendall thinks opening up to others by sharing an embarrassing story about yourself is okay.

'It is not recommended that you begin by making jokes about someone else,' she says, sounding increasingly like a prim, rather than square, teacher. Lots of comics I know are actually very rude, indeed rather abrasive people

---

[178] **Afterword**. Wikihow 31 August 2022

(exchanges online often start with four-letter word rebuffs and maybe abruptly end too with other four-letter word put-downs!) But Kendall's earnest advice is to avoid forms of "low comedy" such as mocking someone's physical appearance or shortcomings, oppressed groups. Women and minorities, people with physical or mental disabilities, and avoid references to bodily functions and sex. No, really, that's the advice. Maybe this more genteel kind of wit is because Kendall is American. Humor is a serious business to be conducted seriously. It is as Mark van Doren (poet, writer, and long-time professor of English at Columbia University) once put it: 'Nothing in man is more serious than his sense of humor; it is the sign that he wants all the truth…'

That's a much-quoted line, which comes from an essay one Mark van Doren wrote about the German writer Thomas Mann. The less often noted part of the essay goes on to say:

'…and sees more sides of it than can be soberly and systematically stated; it is a sign, furthermore, that he can remember one idea even while he entertains another, and that he can live with contradiction. It is the reason, at any rate, that we cannot take seriously one whose mind and heart have never been known to smile.'[179]

But back to Kendall's professional guide, having ruled out most forms of what Freud called "tendentious" humor, she allows a little back in saying you can continue to make fun of yourself! (Genius stuff, this.) Then, and only then "If you are with someone who is able to laugh at themselves, you can gently poke fun at them after you have done the same to yourself. People will begin laughing, and their social anxiety will be reduced."

Yes, ma'am!

Kendall cautions, however, that even self-deprecating jokes *can* make others feel uncomfortable. Stick with something that tastes good.

That's the content, side sorted. What about delivery? The tip here is to 'work on your timing.' This, at least, is apolitical. Keep jokes short and simple, make witty comments at the right moment, not a few minutes later (that rules me out!), and above all, punctuate your own jokes with anticipatory pauses. We might remember from chapter seven that this was one of the things that Ronald Reagan was so good at.

---

[179] POV August 30 2016

Another tip is to target only well-known subjects that won't be harmed. 'Poking fun at authority figures, such as politicians, celebrities, or (former) bosses, is usually safe' says Kendall, who maybe is relying a bit here on the word "usually" as she surely knows that authority figures do not have a sense of humor, and even if occasionally they do, they do not like other people poking fun at them. The world is not very democratic on this, which is why lots of people lose jobs or promotions simply for having the temerity to make a little bit of fun of the boss. And maybe that's why stand-up comedy remains a fringe activity.

Nonetheless, the idea that you "punch up" rather than down is surely right, even if nowadays the range of politically incorrect targets would, if followed, pretty much destroy comedy. "Making fun of a person or entity that lacks power, e.g., an oppressed group, is punching down. Punching up challenges the status quo, while punching it down reinforces it."

More positively, Kendall advises us to remember that laughter is contagious, so if you carry yourself in an open and humorous way, people will be ready to laugh. To break the ice, try smiling and laughing more.

Her last tip is to look for humor in everyday events. Many comedians focus on the world around them to find comedic material. Others look to their past experiences, such as their childhood or past relationships, as a way to make people laugh. Try keeping a diary of funny things that happen to you.

And if, despite doing all this, you're still not all that funny, well, don't give up! Because there is one last strategy left. This is seeking out someone else who is funny (at least in your opinion) and trying to learn from them. Mind you, since Kendall herself warned against copying and inauthenticity, clearly this has to be a bit of a desperate last option. Certainly, I would hate to have to copy Kendall's routine.

Seriously, though, Kendall left me a bit dissatisfied, and I was very pleased to have an actual head-to-head with Dominic Frisby, a British author, voice actor, financial affairs commentator, and comedian. It is in this capacity that he began performing live comedy in 1997, starting as a character comic with "The Upper-Class Rapper", before moving on to observational comedy and compering. He has also appeared in TV sitcoms and experimental comedies. All of which is quite a mix.

Embracing the spirit of variety, Frisby adds songs to his routines. One such is "Ode to the Compost Bin", which he first played in the London club

'Comedy Unleashed.' It's a song offered to show the value of self-interest and how it benefits all participants, through the example of a compost bin:

'They tirelessly process the peel and the rind/with nothing but their self-interest in mind. Nothing is wasted or centrally planned. It's like Adam Smith's invisible hand.'[180]

This is a comedy for graduates. Steve Bennet, founder of the comedy website *Chortle*, which issues annual awards to the best stand-up comics in the UK, characterized his character comedy, such as "Upper-Class Rapper" and "Ludwig the Bavarian", as a string of one-liners, adding that although some gags were "inspired", the overall effect was "sadly patchy", maybe that's why, revisiting his work three years later, Bennet found Frisby had moved on from being a character comic to instead base his routine on real life.

Perhaps he recalled that Henri Bergson wrote that laughter is always connected to humans or to something that can in turn be connected to humans. And that 'A landscape may be beautiful, inviting, magnificent, drab, or repulsive, but it is never funny…'

Anyway, you can't get more real than money. In 2016, Frisby appeared at the Edinburgh Festival Fringe with a show called, practically, if dauntingly, 'Let's Talk About Tax.' The website *FringeReview* called it a 'thoroughly enlightening hour of education and entertainment,' but *The Times* said, 'It's not very funny,' and *The List* found it "took stamina" to keep up with. Perhaps unsurprisingly, it seems that jokes about tax matters haven't quite hit the sweet spot for most people.

Or maybe it's about creating the right context. In conversation, Frisby emphasized to me again and again the joke-making context. Get people in the right mood, and yes, tax affairs too become funny. In his own routines, he starts with some prepared material, precisely to try to create the "joke-making" environment. A lot of the jokes that follow, apparently spontaneously, are still old ones, read or used before, but to some extent, Frisby is also ad-libbing, and on a good night, it becomes hard to know exactly where the jokes come from, but rather they seem to appear spontaneously, helped by the buzz of the occasion and audience. Frisby compares the audience to the music track in a song—switch it off (a joke falls flat), and it's the end of the song too.

---

[180] Frisby 2020

'This is the dynamic of comedy clubs: the audience is part of the show. The audience track is part of the rhythm of an act. It's like the audience is the music track. So, the comedian brings his act, but the audience brings the laughter, and the two go together, and that's how comedy is created.'

It's still highly social, as Frisby says:

'I don't think any comedian goes on stage thinking in terms of anthropological processes or whatever is going on with laughter. He has an act that hopefully he has learned and honed, and he just goes onstage hoping to perform the act as well as he can.'

When a comic is on stage, he or she has to be in the moment. At the same time, all the improvised comedy is improvised around structure.

'Almost all the time, comedians have been in that moment sometime before, so they know how to handle it, and a lot of improvised comedy is not as improvised as it looks.'

Comics are funny because they have learned their material. But it's definitely not a complicated theory. However, there's a problem with rehearsing routines and learning material, which is that humor dates more than any other art form. Frisby again:

'If you look at Shakespeare, his plays stand up, but the histories and tragedies are better than the comedies, let alone the "bawdy word play". I mean, no one understands what they are talking about! It might have been hilarious at the time, but no one understands it now. Partly the meanings of words change, but also the inferences, the references, and the cultural context are different. The result is that nowadays actors performing Shakespeare think they have to grab their crotches all the time to demonstrate that they are talking about something bawdy. But that's just vulgar and cheap; it's not funny.'

This peculiar time-specific character of humor helps explain why sitcoms date a lot more than other forms of comedy, while other forms, particularly wordplay—the meaning of words, double meanings—seem to age better. On the other hand, says Frisby, if you have a comedy that is more about a situation—like the theatrical farce of Basil Fawlty, the proprietor of a seaside English hotel in the TV sitcom *Fawlty Towers*, trying to hide a dead body from the other guests—it seems to stay funnier ever better than wordplay! Perhaps it's because in scenes like these, Fawlty loses his ability to control events; he becomes, like the body of the dead guest, an object. All of which echoes another of Henri Bergson's theories, notably that aspect he calls "mechanical inelasticity", which he makes central to understanding what makes things funny. Bergson sees humor emerging in the transformation of someone from a controlling actor in an event to an object, which is also something that Charlie Chaplin and Buster Keaton films play on all the time.

But those exceptional cases aside, as TV schedulers know, the short version of it is that comedy dates.

Comperes like Frisby and stand-up comics in general are well aware that, as we saw Freud put it earlier, we laugh 'by ricochet.' As Freud recalls the words of Louis Dugas in the 1902 book '*La Psychologie du Rire*':

'Laughter belongs to those manifestations of psychic states that are highly infectious.'[181]

A simple experiment by a team of researchers from Goldsmiths and Birkbeck Colleges in London demonstrated this very well in 2018.[182] A group of young children, aged between two and four years old, were shown comic clips under three different conditions: individually, in pairs, or in groups of six or eight. When the children watched the cartoons on their own, they remained expressionless. When they watched them in pairs or groups, though, they rolled around laughing. So humor is definitely a communal thing, and smiles and laughter are primarily social signals rather than any actual reflexive response to humor.

How important is that Ah-ha moment in humor, the aspect that impressed Freud so much, compared to simple delight in predictable routines? Frisby thinks novelty is part of being funny, and yet those routines also serve to create the right context for laughter. We enjoy the lead-up to a joke sometimes more than the joke itself, while, particularly in comedy clubs, swearing and vulgarity are tools used by the comics to enhance the effect of routines.

Many comedians and many sitcoms are accused of relying on stereotypes and aggressive jokes at the expense of targeted minorities. As we saw in chapter two, some see aggressive intent in the most innocuous themes, such as the series of apparently harmless jokes about elephants standing on marshmallows, which sociologists have linked to racism in America. Frisby, however, rejects the claim that all jokes conceal hidden aggressive intent. 'How is someone like Tim Vine doing puns aggressive?' he asks. For those outside the profession, I should explain that Tim Vine is another British

---

[181] Freud 1922 242)

[182] Andyman et al 2018

comedian who won the award for "Best Joke" not once but twice at the Edinburgh Fringe. Two of his winning jokes were, one: 'I've just been on a once-in-a-lifetime holiday. I'll tell you what, never again,' and two: 'I decided to sell my Hoover. Well, it was just collecting dust.' Neither of these "award-winning" jokes are puns, but they're far from aggressive either.

For Frisby, there are far too many examples of jokes that are not aggressive enough for a theory based on that to work. That said, he thinks a lot of humor is borne out of anger, including some of the best wit. 'The comedy of custard pie is somebody exploiting aggression to derive laughter,' he says.

Instead, in Frisby's view, humor is highly subjective, and while loads of people have tried to dissect comedy and explain how it works, they've all failed, because it's a moving target, and situations and values all change.

Add to which, Frisby points out that the perspective of academic observers on actual practitioners—comedians—is very different. Only the latter really appreciates the importance of delivery, lightness of touch, a certain voice, and even having a certain appearance.

Let's give the final word to him, a professional comic.

'There are a gazillion kinds of comedy, from sketch shows to sitcoms to storytelling to stand up; I wouldn't try to find a none-size-fits-all rule to explain them. And yet, most comedians will ultimately acknowledge the importance of the jokes, saying that you're only as good as your material.'

Which is why we will now finish this chapter with a joke. And here it is:

What do you get when you cross a joke with a rhetorical question?

Sources and Suggestions for Further Reading

ABC News 2005. No author. 'Sound of Dog's "Laugh" Calms Other Pooches'. https://abcnews.go.com/GMA/Health/story?id=1370911 Accessed October 1 2022.

Abrahams, Roger D. "18. On Elephantasy and Elephanticide". *Analytic Essays in Folklore*, Berlin, Boston: De Gruyter Mouton, 2019, pp. 192–205. https://doi.org/10.1515/9783110903768-021

Addyman, Caspar & Fogelquist, Charlotte & Levakova, Lenka & Rees, Sarah. (2018). Social Facilitation of Laughter and Smiles in Preschool Children. *Frontiers in Psychology*. 9. 10.3389/fpsyg.2018.01048.

Alvarado, G. E. (2013). *Gallows Humor as a Resiliency Factor Among Urban Firefighters with Specific Implications on Prevalence Rates of PTSD*. Azusa: Azusa Pacific University

American Kennel Club. March 27, 2020. 'Do Dogs Have a Sense of Humor?' By Jan Reisen. https://www.akc.org/expert-advice/lifestyle/do-dogs-have-a-sense-of-humor/ Accessed October 1 2022.

Americanisraelite.com February 4 2021. No author. https://www.americanisraelite.com/arts_and_entertainment/joke_of_the_wee k/article_de3346ee-6584-11eb-bb68-5b5367ca4dcd.html

Aristotle, *Poetics*. Trans. S. H. Butcher. http://classics.mit.edu//Aristotle/poetics.html Accessed September 9 2022.

Aristotle, *Rhetoric*. 'On Poetry and Style'. Translated by W. Rhys Roberts http://classics.mit.edu/Aristotle/rhetoric.html

Attarwala, T. 2010, 'TGN1412: From Discovery to Disaster'. *Journal of Young Pharmacists*, 2010 Jul;2(3):332–6

AWI Animal Welfare Institute. AWI Quarterly Winter 2011 Do Animals Have a Sense of Humor?

https://awionline.org/awi-quarterly/2011-winter/do-animals-have-sense-humor

Bailly, Lioner et al. 2018. *The Lacan Tradition*. Abingdon: Routledge.

BenLewisProjects.com By Ben Lewis. 22 July, 2007. "Stalin Jokes". https://benlewisprojects.com/blog/jokes/stalin-jokes

Bergson, Henri (1911) *Laughter, an Essay on the Meaning of the Comic.* Translation by Cloudesley Barenton and Fred Rothwell. https://www.templeofearth.com/books/laughter.pdf

Bergson, Henri. 1912. *Laughter, An Essay on the Meaning of the Comic.* Project Gutenberg: https://www.gutenberg.org/ebooks/4352 Accessed September 20 2022.

Bestjokehub, no date, no author. Teacher: "Anyone who thinks they're stupid, stand up!" https://bestjokehub.com/joke-94779/ Accessed September 20 2022.

Bestjokehub.com. No author, no date. Joke-9901: "A frightened man goes to the secret police and says, 'My talking parrot disappeared'." https://bestjokehub.com/joke-9901/ Accessed September 20 2022.

de Bono, Edward. *Lateral Thinking for Management: a handbook.* 1982. New York: Penguin

Bor, Daniel. 2012. *The Ravenous Brain: How the New Science of Consciousness Explains Our Insatiable Search for Meaning.* New York: Basic Books.

Boston Globe. By David Mehegan, August 15, 2007. "Sharing laughs and a love of philosophy." http://archive.boston.com/news/globe/living/articles/2007/08/15/sharing_laughs_and_a_love_of_philosophy/ accessed September 9, 2022

BrainyQuote, no date. "Emo Philips Quotes". https://www.brainyquote.com/quotes/emo_philips_128947Accessed September 20 2022.

Bressler, E. R., Martin, R. A., & Balshine, S. (2006). "Production and appreciation of humor as sexually selected traits". *Evolution and Human Behavior*, 27(2), 121–130. https://doi.org/10.1016/ j.evolhumbehav.2005.09.001

Brunvand, Jan Harold 2011. *Too Good to Be True: The Colossal Book of Urban Legends*. New York: W. W. Norton

Bunnin, Nicholas and Tsui-James, Eric 2008. *The Blackwell Companion to Philosophy.*

https://www.perlego.com/book/2777684/the-blackwell-companion-to-philosophy-pdf

Carroll, Lewis. *Through the Looking Glass*. Project Gutenberg: https://www.gutenberg.org/files/12/12-0.txt Accessed September 20 2022.

Cathcart, Thomas and Klein, Daniel. 2008. *Plato and a Platypus Walk into a Bar: Understanding Philosophy Through Jokes*. New York: Penguin.

Cato.org. By Vladimir Bukovsky. December 18 2005. "Torture's Long Shadow". https://www.cato.org/commentary/tortures-long-shadow Accessed September 20 2022.

Chan, Y.-C., Liao, Y.-J., Tu, C.-H., & Chen, H.-C. (2016). "Neural correlates of hostile jokes: Cognitive and motivational processes in humor appreciation". *Frontiers in Human Neuroscience*, 10, Article 527. https://doi.org/10.3389/fnhum.2016.00527

Chang, Yi-Tzu; Ku, Li-Chuan; Chen, Hsueh-Chih (2018) "Sex differences in humor processing: An event-related potential study". *Brain and Cognition*, Volume 120, Pages 34–42, ISSN 0278-2626, https://doi.org/10.1016/j.bandc.2017.11.002. https:// www.sciencedirect.com/science/article/pii/S027826261730283X

Christopher, Sarah. December 2015. "An introduction to black humor as a coping mechanism for student paramedics". *Journal of Paramedic Practice.* 7(12):610–615 DOI: 10.12968/jpar.2015.7.12.610. https://www.researchgate.net/publication/285582173_An_introduction_to_bl ack_humor_as_a_coping_mechanism_for_student_paramedics

Cicero, *De Oratore*, 2.217 Translated by J. S. Watson http://attalus.org/cicero/deoratore2C.html

Cohen, Martin. 2007. *101 Philosophy Problems* (3rd edition). London: Routledge.

Collider.com (April 6, 2022) "The 9 Best Late Night TV Hosts Currently on Air", by Shawn Van Horn. https://collider.com/best-late-night-tv-hosts-currently-on-air/Accessed October 16 2022.

Commentary. November 1964. "The Act of Creation, by Arthur Koestler". https://www.commentary.org/articles/kathleen-nott/the-act-of-creation-by-arthur-koestler/ Accessed September 24 2022.

ConstitutionCenter.org. "Looking back: George Carlin and the Supreme Court". By Bomboy, Scott. July 3, 2022.
https://constitutioncenter.org/blog/george-carlin-and-the-supreme-court
Accessed September 20 2022.

Cooper, Tommy. *All In One Joke Book: Book Joke, Joke Book.* 2014. Cedar Rapids: Arrow.

Cray, Ed and Herzog, Marilyn Eisenberg. "The Absurd Elephant: A Recent Riddle Fad". Western Folklore. Vol. 26, No. 1 (January 1967), pp. 27–36 online at https://www.jstor.org/stable/1498485

*Daily Mail.*2022. "The comedy (stealing) club". By James Robinson. November 3rd 2022.
https://www.dailymail.co.uk/news/article-11385711/The-comedy-stealing-club-James-Corden-joins-list-stand-ups-accused-pinching-skits.html
Accessed November 3rd 2022,

Darwin, Charles. 1872. *On the Expression of Emotions in Man and Animals.* London: John Murray. Online at:
https://brocku.ca/MeadProject/Darwin/Darwin_1872_05.html

Draenos, Stan. "Psychoanalysis, Evolution and the End of Metaphysics". Σπύρος Δραῖνας. *Canadian Journal of Social and Political Theory.* Volume 2 Number 2, Spring-Summer 1978.

Epicurus. *Lives of the Philosophers*, Letter to Menoeceus.
https://blogs.ubc.ca/phil102/files/2018/02/Epicurus-LtrMenoeceus-epicurusinfo.pdf Accessed September 9 2022

Exploringyourmind.com 13 November 2021. "Do Animals Have a Sense of Humor? Science Says Yes." No author. https://exploringyourmind.com/do-animals-have-a-sense-of-humor-science-says-yes/ Accessed October 1 2022.

Farley, Christopher. 1999, "Seriously Funny". *Time.* September 5 1999.
http://content.time.com/time/magazine/article/0,9171,30524,00.html
Accessed September 6 2022

Feig K (1979) *Hitler's Death Camps: The Sanity of Madness.* Holmes and Meier, New York

Feld.com No author. September 22 2005. "Joke Of The Day: How Many Is A Brazillion?" https://feld.com/archives/2005/09/joke-of-the-day-how-many-is-a-brazillion/ Accessed September 20 2022.

FilmReference.com. "How I Learned To Stop Worrying And Love The Bomb". No date. By Gene Phillips. http://www.filmreference.com/Films-De-Dr/Dr-Strangelove-Or-How-I-Learned-to-Stop-Worrying-and-Love-the-Bomb.html Accessed October 18 2022.

FindLaw.com, no date. No author. "FCC v. PACIFICA FOUNDATION". https://caselaw.findlaw.com/us-supreme-court/438/726.html
Accessed September 20, 2022.

Foucault, Michel. *Madness and Civilization: A History of Madness in the Age of Reason.* Translated by Richard Howard. New York: Vintage Books, 1988.

Free-funny-jokes.com. "Sartre's Coffee Joke". No date, no author. https://free-funny-jokes.com/sartres-coffee/ Accessed September 20 2022.

Freud, Sigmund. 1922. *Wit and Its Relation to the Unconscious.* London: Kegan Paul.
https://ia803401.us.archive.org/8/items/wit-and-its-relation-to-the-unconscious/Wit%20and%20its%20relation%20to%20the%20unconscious.pdf

Frisby, Dominic 2020. "DEBT BOMB—The Global Financial Crisis Stripped Bare" 3 minutes 30 seconds.
https://www.youtube.com/watch?v=GXcLVDhS8fM. Accessed September 28 2022.

Frisby, Dominic 2022. Interview by author, Normandy, 7 July 2022.

futilitycloset.com. November 19 2005. "An International Riddle".
https://www.futilitycloset.com/2005/11/19/an-international-riddle/ Accessed September 28 2022.

Gifford, Ron. "Humor, creativity and the analytical mind" TEDx lecture, Carmel High School 23 June 2013.
https://www.youtube.com/watch?v=SJjKv-hYmzY Accessed September 24 2022.

Goldstein E. Bruce (2010). *Encyclopedia of Perception.* Atlanta: Sage Publications.

Goodman, Lizbeth (1992) "Gender and humor". In: Bonnet, Goodman, Allen, Janes and King, editors: *Imagining women: Cultural representations and gender.* 296–300. Cambridge: Polity.

The Guardian, 7 July 2022. "Sacha Baron Cohen defeats Roy Moore's $95m lawsuit over 'pedophile detector'" https://www.theguardian.com/culture/2022/jul/07/sacha-baron-cohen-defeats-roy-moore-lawsuit?amp;amp;amp Accessed September 20 2022.

Harvard.edu. No author, no date. "Harvard Project on the Soviet Social System: Transcripts and notes from 705 interviews with Soviet refugees in the early Cold War era." https://library.harvard.edu/collections/harvard-project-soviet-social-system Accessed September 20 2022.

Hazlitt, William (1819). *Lectures on the English Comic Writers* 'On Wit and Humor.' New York: Wiley.

Heisenberg, Werner. 1958, *Physics and Philosophy: The Revolution in Modern Science.* New York: Harper & Row.

Hetzron, Robert (1991). "On the structure of punchlines". *Humor: International Journal of Humor Research.* 4 (1)

Hierocles 1983. *The Philogelos, Or, Laughter Lover* Amsterdam: J. C. Gieben. (The barber joke is no. 56 in the collection of 265.)

Hillenbrand F. K. M. *Underground Humor In Nazi Germany, 1933–1945.* New York: Routledge 1995.

Hobbes, Thomas. 1650, *Leviathan.* "Human Nature" Ch. 9, sect. 13 Project Gutenberg: https://www.gutenberg.org/files/3207/3207-h/3207-h.htm Accessed September 10 2022.

Hofmann, Jennifer; Platt, Tracey; Lau, Chloe; Torres-Marín, Jorge (2020) "Gender differences in humor-related traits, humor appreciation, production, comprehension, (neural) responses, use, and correlates: A systematic review" *Current Psychology.* DOI: https://doi.org/10.1007/ s12144-020-00724-1.

*Holistic Nursing Practic*e 1996 Jan;10(2):49–56. Doi: 10.1097/00004650-199601000-00007. Humor: an antidote for stress. By P. Wooten PMID: 8550690 DOI: 10.1097/00004650-199601000-00007.

Houser, Nathan and Ktoesel, Christian. 1992 *The Essential Peirce, Volume 1: Selected Philosophical Writings (1867–1893).* Bloomington: Indiana University Press.

Howrigan, Daniel and MacDonald, Kevin 2008. "Humor as a Mental Fitness Indicator". *Evolutionary Psychology*, Volume: 6 issue: 4, online only. https://doi.org/10.1177/147470490800600411

HuffPost.com By Makini Brice (via Reuters). March 4 2018 "At Gridiron Dinner, Trump Says He 'Won't Rule Out Direct Talks With Kim Jong Un'." https://www.huffpost.com/entry/trump-gridiron-north-korea_n_5a9bb85de4b0479c025345fc Accessed September 20 2022.

HuffPost.com By Steven Hoffer. October 9 2016. 'Billy Bush Suspended From The "Today" Show'. https://www.huffpost.com/entry/billy-bush-today-show-apology_n_57fa836ae4b0e655eab53813

HuffPost.com By Ryan J. Reilly. July 28, 2017. "Donald Trump Endorses Police Brutality In Speech To Cops". Accessed September 20 2022.

Hume, David. *A Treatise of Human Nature*. Reprinted, L.A. Selby-Bigge (ed.), Oxford: Clarendon Press. Hume 1738 [1896] available online. https://oll.libertyfund.org/title/bigge-a-treatise-of-human-nature

Humoropedia.com No author, no date. "33 Funny Russian Jokes and Puns" https://humoropedia.com/funny-russian-jokes-n-puns/ Accessed September 20 2022.

Hurley Matthew, Dennett, Daniel and Adams, Reginald. (2011) *Inside Jokes: Using Humor to Reverse-Engineer the Mind*. Cambridge, Massachusetts MIT Press.

I-*d Magazine* August 7 2018. "The feminist comedians dismantling sexist 'jokes'". By El Hunt. https://i-d.vice.com/en/article/xwk58a/hannah-gadsby-nanette-ali-wong-naomi-ekperigin-the-feminist-comedians-dismantling-sexist-jokes Accessed September 20 2022.

Internet Archive. No date. The Act of Creation, Arthur Koestler.pdf https://archive.org/stream/pdfy-rDIHDXbS3uvtgXcr/The+Act+of+Creation%2C+Arthur+Koestler_djvu.txt

JapanTimes.co.jp by Dan Hill. June 11 2015. "Russian president's secrets are right on his face". https://www.japantimes.co.jp/opinion/2015/06/11/commentary/world-commentary/russian-presidents-secrets-are-right-on-his-face/Accessed September 20 2022.

Jelavich, Peter. 2021. Chapter 8, "Cabaret under National Socialism." In *Berlin Cabaret*, 228–257. Cambridge, MA and London, England: Harvard University Press, 2021

Jokes Blogger. No author, no date. "Joke of the Day: Old lady in bank". https://www.jokesblogger.com/2014/05/16/joke-of-the-day-old-lady-in-bank/ Jokes-just-for-fun.blogspot.com No author, no date. "Stalin And Zhukov Meeting." https://jokes-just-for-fun.blogspot.com/2017/08/stalin-and-zhukov-meeting.html Accessed September 20 2022.

jokes4all.net no author, no date. "Pig Jokes: Top 10 Jokes about Pigs" https://jokes4all.net/pig-jokes Accessed September 20 2022.

jokesoftheday.net no author, no date. http://www.jokesoftheday.net/joke-Elephants-and-Marshmallows/201302241 Accessed September 20 2022.

Knutson B, Burgdorf J, Panksepp J. Anticipation of play elicits high-frequency ultrasonic vocalizations in young rats. Journal of Comparative Psychology. 1998 Mar;112(1):65–73. Doi: 10.1037/0735-7036.112.1.65. PMID: 9528115.

Kobassa S, Puccetti M (1983) "Personality and social resources in stress resistance." *Journal of Personal and Social Psychology* 45(4): 839–50.

Koestler, Arthur. 1940. *Darkness at Noon*. New York: Macmillan.

Koko.org March 18 2010. 'Gorillas just wanna have fun,' by Gary Stanley. https://www.koko.org/research-care/802/gorillas-just-wanna-have-fun/) Accessed October 1 2022.

Lampert, Martina and Ervin-Tripp, Susan (1998) "Exploring paradigms: The study of gender and sense of humor near the end of the 20th century" *Education* DOI:10.1515/9783110804607.231 Corpus ID: 192110017

Lancaster University, no author no date. "Chuckle Stoop". Accessed September 10 2022. https://www.lancaster.ac.uk/fass/projects/stylistics/topic3a/fun4.htm

LennyBruce.org, no date, no author. https://lennybruce.org/2022/06/28/arrest-that-joke-a-history-of-gags-so-offensive-that-punters-called-the-cops-the-guardian/

Lewis, Ben 2011. *Hammer And Tickle: A History Of Communism Told Through Communist Jokes*. Cambridge: Pegasus 2010

Lincoln, Kenneth. 1993. *Indi'n Humor: Bicultural Play in Native America*. Oxford: Oxford University Press.

Logan, Brian. 28 June 2022. "Arrest that joke! A history of gags so offensive that punters called the cops". *The Guardian*.

https://www.theguardian.com/stage/2022/jun/28/arrest-joke-history-gags-offensive-punters-cops-police-joe-lycett-sacha-baron-cohen-jo-brand Accessed September 20 2022.

Lorenz, Konrad 2002 "Man Meets Dog" London: Routledge. ISBN 9780415267458.

Ma, Moses. "The Power of Humor in Ideation and Creativity". June 12 2014. *Psychology Today.* https://www.psychologytoday.com/us/blog/the-tao-innovation/201406/the-power-humor-in-ideation-and-creativity Accessed September 24 2022.

Malcolm, Norman, *Ludwig Wittgenstein: A Memoir.* Oxford: Clarendon Press. (The exact phrase is "once said that a serious and good philosophical work could be written that would consist entirely of jokes".)

Martin, D. M., Rich, C. O., & Gayle, B. M. (2004). "Humor works: Communication style and humor functions in manager/subordinate relationships". *Southern Communication Journal*, 69, 206–222.

Martin, Rod. "Do Children Laugh Much More Often than Adults Do?". *Association for Applied and Therapeutic Humor.* https://aath.memberclicks.net/do-children-laugh-much-more-often-than-adults-do Accessed September 24 2022.

Mejokes.com No author, no date. No title. https://mejokes.com/stalins-ghost/ Accessed September 20 2022.

Mentalfloss.com No author. February 28, 2018. Alvin Ward. "What Is the Car's Parking Spot Number?" https://www.mentalfloss.com/article/533625/parking-spot-brain-teaser

Mill, 1897. *Early Essays of John Stuart Mill*, edited by J. W. M. Gibbs. London: George Bell and Sons. https://archive.org/stream/nd988095368/004600654_djvu.txt Accessed September 20 2022.

Milton, John and Carruthers, Robert. *The Poetry of Milton's Prose: Selected from His Various Writings, with Notes, and an Introductory Essay.* United Kingdom: Longman, Rees, Orme, Brown, and Green, 1827.

The Modern Psychologist, n.d., "Nagel and Camus on the Absurd" by Brad Peters. Online at https://modernpsychologist.ca/nagel-and-camus-on-the-absurd/

Monroe, Mary. 2012. *Deliver Me from Evil.* Chapter 24. New York: Kensington Books.

Moran C (1990) Does the use of humor as a coping strategy affect stresses associated with emergency work? *International Journal of Mass Emergency Disasters* 8(3): 361–77

Mythologyexplained.com No date. No author. "The Sphinx Riddle: The Story of Oedipus and the Sphinx in Greek Mythology" https://mythologyexplained.com/oedipus-and-the-sphinx-riddle/

Nagel, Thomas. "The Absurd". *Journal of Philosophy*, Vol. 68, No. 20, Sixty-Eighth Annual Meeting of the American Philosophical Association Eastern Division (Oct. 21, 1971), pp. 716–727 http://www.jstor.org/stable/2024942. Accessed: 17/09/2022

The New Republic. "No one wants to defend Roy Moore for allegedly courting underage girls. Except Breitbart." Jeet Heer, November 9, 2017. https://newrepublic.com/minutes/145770/no-one-wants-defend-roy-moore-allegedly-courting-underage-girls-except-breitbart Accessed September 20 2022

New York Post. By Ebony Bowden. "Trump claims disinfectant remarks were sarcastic questions to reporters." https://nypost.com/2020/04/24/trump-claims-disinfectant-remarks-were-sarcastic-question-to-reporters/Accessed September 20 2022.

New York Times 1964. Knickerbocker, C., Humor with a Mortal Sting in New York Times Book Review, September 27 1964, Sec. 7. https://www.nytimes.com/1964/09/27/archives/humor-with-a-mortal-sting.html

New York Times. September 5 2006. "Dogs May Laugh, but Only Cats Get the Joke". by James Gorman. https://www.nytimes.com/2006/09/05/science/05side.html

New York Times, Oct 11 2013: "Comic's talk show takes a risk: common ground" by Maureen Dowd. https://www.nytimes.com/2013/11/10/opinion/sunday/dowd-funny-girl.html Accessed September 20 2022

New York Times, archive, December 1 1973. "3 Dozen American Journalists Are Said to Do Work for C.I.A".

https://www.nytimes.com/1973/12/01/archives/3-dozen-american-journalists-are-said-to-do-work-for-cia.html Accessed September 20 2022

The New Yorker. Adam Kirsch. September 23 2019. "The Desperate Plight Behind 'Darkness at Noon'."
https://www.newyorker.com/magazine/2019/09/30/the-desperate-plight-behind-darkness-at-noon Accessed September 20 2022

The New Yorker. By Emily Nussbaum. January 23, 2017 "How Jokes Won the Election: How do you fight an enemy who's just kidding?"
https://www.newyorker.com/magazine/2017/01/23/how-jokes-won-the-election Accessed September 20 2022.

News.com.au Via Agence France Press. November 25, 2016. "Putin jokes: 'Russia's borders don't end anywhere'" Accessed September 20 2022.

Newsweek.com. By Isabel van Brugen. March 18 2022 "Vladimir Putin Suddenly Disappears From TV Broadcast During Russia Speech".
https://www.newsweek.com/vladimir-putin-suddenly-disappears-mid-speech-russia-tv-broadcast-1689443 Accessed September 20 2022.

News.ycombinator.com. By bifrost. February 6, 2017. "CIA Declassified Coldwar Russian Jokes". https://news.ycombinator.com/item?id=13585511 Accessed September 20 2022.

Nicholson, Christie. 2012. "The Humor Gap". *Scientific American*. October 1 2012.
https://www.scientificamerican.com/article/the-humor-gap-2012-10-23/ Accessed September 6 2022

Nietzsche, Friedrich. 1998. *Beyond Good and Evil*. Oxford: Oxford University Press.

Nugent, Annable. "Judd Apatow backtracks controversial comments about Will Smith hitting Chris Rock". *The Independent*. March 29 2022.
https://www.independent.co.uk/arts-entertainment/films/news/judd-apatow-will-smith-chris-rock-comments-b2046316.html Accessed September 20 2022

Oring, Elliott, 2010. *Engaging Humor*. Champaign: University of Illinois Press

Orwell.ru. Orwell George. No date. *The Art of Donald McGill*.
https://www.orwell.ru/library/reviews/McGill/english/e_mcgill Accessed September 10 2022.

Orwell.ru. Orwell, George. July 28, 1945. "Funny, but not Vulgar".

https://orwell.ru/library/articles/funny/english/e_funny Accessed September 20 2022

Ostrower C (1998) "Humor as a defense mechanism in the holocaust". https://www.academia.edu/554260/Humor_as_a_Defense_Mechanism_in_the_Holocaust Accessed September 10 2022

PBS.org July 31 2017 By Associated Press. Trump was "making a joke" in don't-be-too-nice police speech, White House says. https://www.pbs.org/newshour/politics/trump-making-joke-dont-nice-police-speech-white-house-says Accessed September 20 2022.

PBS.org September 24 2000. No author. "The Reagan/Mondale Debates". https://www.pbs.org/newshour/spc/debatingourdestiny/doc1984.html Accessed September 23 2022.

Peirce, Charles (1891) *Collected Papers* https://edisciplinas.usp.br/pluginfile.php/5165117/mod_resource/content/0/The%20Collected%20Papers%20of%20Charles%20Sanders%20Peirce%20%282904s%29.pdf Accessed September 23 2022.

Plato, *Phaedo*. Project Gutenberg: https://www.gutenberg.org/files/1658/1658-h/1658-h.htm Accessed September 10 2022

POV (Point of View Magazine). "Reality Laughs: Looking for Comedy in the Documentary World". By Liam Lacey. https://povmagazine.com/reality-laughs-looking-for-comedy-in-the-documentary-world/ Accessed September 28 2022.

Prospect. Ben Lewis. May 20 2006. "Hammer & tickle". https://www.prospectmagazine.co.uk/magazine/communist-jokes Accessed September 23 2022

PsychCentral. "How and Why Humor Differs Between the Sexes". Nichole Force. https://psychcentral.com/lib/how-and-why-humor-differs-between-the-sexes#1 Accessed September 6 2022

Psycho-tests.com. "Humor Styles Questionnaire". Psycho-tests.com. https://psycho-tests.com/test/humor-styles-questionnaire. Accessed 6/9/2022

PuzzleWocky.com No author, no date. "Situation Puzzles". https://puzzlewocky.com/brain-teasers/situation-puzzles/

189

Quora.com, Cody Woods, no date. "What are common topics and themes in stand-up comedy?" https://www.quora.com/What-are-common-topics-and-themes-in-standup-comedy Accessed September 20 2022.

Rayner, Jay. 25 July 1999. "The Jesus Christ of stand-up". *The Guardian*. https://www.theguardian.com/lifeandstyle/1999/jul/25/foodanddrink.comedy Accessed September 20 2022.

Radio Canada (RCI). October 29 2021. "Comedian who mocked disabled child singer did not breach limits of free speech: Supreme Court". https://ici.radio-canada.ca/rci/en/news/1835551/comedian-who-mocked-disabled-child-singer-did-not-breach-limits-of-free-speech-supreme-court Accessed September 20 2022.

Reagan.com No author. April 15 2019. "Tax Day & Ronald Reagan Tax Cutting Legacy". https://www.reagan.com/tax-day-ronald-reagan-tax-cutting-legacy-reagancom Accessed September 23 2022.

Reaganlibrary.gov No author. April 18 1988. "Remarks at a White House Meeting With the Associated General Contractors of America". https://www.reaganlibrary.gov/archives/speech/remarks-white-house-meeting-associated-general-contractors-america-0 Accessed September 23 2022.

Reuters. By Reuters staff. October 4 2017. "Boris Johnson jokes about dead bodies in Libya". https://www.reuters.com/article/uk-britain-politics-libya-idUKKCN1C82RU Accessed September 20 2022.

RobertHalf.com 2017. "Jokes All Around". March 28, 2017. https://www.roberthalf.com/blog/salaries-and-skills/jokes-all-around Accessed 6/9/2022

Rolph, Cecil. H. 1961. *The Trial of Lady Chatterly: Regina V. Penguin Books Limited: The Transcript of the Trial*. New York, Penguin books.

Rosenberg L (1991) A qualitative investigation of the use of humor by emergency personnel as a strategy for coping with stress. *Journal of Emergency Nursing* 17(4): 197–202

Schopenhauer, Arthur (1818) *The World As Will And Idea*, trans. R. Haldane and J. Kemp. Project Gutenberg, https://www.gutenberg.org/files/38427/38427-h/38427-h.html Accessed September 10 2022

Schwehm, Andrew J., McDermut, Wilson, and Thorpe, Katherine. (August 5, 2015) "A gender study of personality and humor in comedians". Humor, https://doi.org/10.1515/humor-2015–0069

Scientific American (2012), "The Humor Gap". Christie Nicholson. October 1 2012.

https://www.scientificamerican.com/article/the-humor-gap-2012-10-23/ Accessed September 6 2022

Scientific American (2019) "What's So Funny? The Science of Why We Laugh: Psychologists, neuroscientists and philosophers are trying to understand humor" By Giovanni Sabato on June 26, 2019

https://www.scientificamerican.com/article/whats-so-funny-the-science-of-why-we-laugh/ Accessed September 6 2022

ScrollDroll.com (2022) "18 Best Stand-Up Comedians In The World Who You Make You Laugh Out Loud" By Simran Martha. (January 10, 2022) https://www.scrolldroll.com/best-stand-up-comedians-in-the-world/ Accessed October 15 2022.

Seals, Monique 2022. "US voices question if Putin underestimated Ukraine". *The Hill.* February 27 2022. https://thehill.com/policy/international/596046-us-voices-question-if-putin-underestimated-ukraine/ Accessed September 6 2022

Simon, Neil. 1973, *The Sunshine Boys: A New Comedy.* New York: Random House

Snopes.com 20 December 1999. "1994s Most Bizarre Suicide".

https://www.snopes.com/fact-check/1994s-most-bizarre-suicide/Accessed September 24 2022.

Sovietjokes.blogspot.com No author. November 11 2021. "Stalin hears a sneeze".

https://sovietjokes.blogspot.com/2021/11/stalin-hears-sneeze.html Accessed September 20 2022.

Starts At 60. July 4, 2018. "Travel at 60 Daily Joke: A man and woman share a sleeper cabin". https://startsat60.com/media/travel/train-joke-two-strangers-share-sleeper-cabin-blanket Accessed September 20 2022.

Sunny Skyz.2013. "Sherlock Holmes and Dr. Watson Go Camping" February 27 2013. https://www.sunnyskyz.com/funny-jokes/20/Sherlock-Holmes-and-Dr.-Watson-Go-Camping Accessed September 10 2022.

"Supreme Court Advance Decisions Volume 60". 1995. No author. Manila, Rex Books.

Tallis, Raymond (2011) *Aping Mankind: Neuromania, Darwinitis and the Misrepresentation of Humanity.* London: Routledge.
Three Quarks Daily. March 21 2016 'The "Streetlight Effect": A Metaphor For Knowledge And Ignorance'. By Yohan John.
https://3quarksdaily.com/3quarksdaily/2016/03/the-streetlight-effect-a-metaphor-for-knowledge-and-ignorance.html Accessed September 10 2022.
Tian F, Hou Y, Zhu W, Dietrich A, Zhang Q, Yang W, Chen Q, Sun J, Jiang Q, Cao G. October 13 2017. "Getting the Joke: Insight during Humor Comprehension—Evidence from an fMRI Study". *Frontiers in Psychology.* October 18 2017.
Time.com September 5 1999. By Christopher John Farley. "Seriously Funny".
http://content.time.com/time/magazine/article/0,9171,30524,00.html Accessed September 20 2022.
Time.com October 22 2010 "Sample Some British Humor! The Official List Of The Best British Jokes" By Frances Perraudin.
https://newsfeed.time.com/2010/10/22/sample-some-british-humor-the-official-list-of-the-best-british-jokes/ Accessed September 20 2022.
Time.com April 18 2019. By Kathy Ehrich Dowd. "President Trump Told Mueller He Was Just Joking When He Asked Russia to Hack Hillary Clinton" https://time.com/5573539/trump-clinton-russia-hack-joke/Accessed September 20 2022.

Ucsd.edu No date. No author. "Let's Make a Deal: Monty Knows". https://mathweb.ucsd.edu/~crypto/Monty/monty.html?_ga=2.73327251.1828 253864.1663673562-1848398046.1663673562
Unification.net. "World Scripture: Tolerance and Respect for All Believers". Udana 68–69. No date, no author.
https://www.unification.net/ws/theme00b.htm Accessed September 22 2022.
Upjoke.com no author, no date. "Beloved jokes". https://upjoke.com/beloved-jokes Accessed September 10 2022.
Upjoke.com, no author, no date. Corn Jokes: Guy goes to a therapist. He says, 'Doc, I live in constant fear that I'm a grain of corn and there's a giant chicken out there who wants to eat me.'

https://upjoke.com/corn-
jokes#:~:text=He%20says%2C%20%22Doc%2C%20I%20live%20in%20co
nstant%20fear,corn%20that%20a%20g
ant%20chicken%20wants%20to%20eat.

Upjoke.com, no author, no date. "Gorbachev jokes".
https://upjoke.com/gorbachev-jokes Accessed September 20 2022.

Upworthy.com 29 November 2022 "A major UCLA study says that at least 65
species of animals laugh" By Annie Reneau. https://www.upworthy.com/new-
study-65-species-animal-laughter-rp Accessed October 1 2022.

Valentine, John. March 1 2012. "Chimpanzee Paintings and the Concept of
Art" in *The Philosopher*, Volume 100 No. 1.
http://www.the-philosopher.co.uk/2012/03/chimpanzee-paintings-and-
concept-of-art.html

Vahshatedil.wordpress.com By Vahshatedil. February 7, 2010. "Another
round of Soviet-era humor II"
https://vahshatedil.wordpress.com/2010/02/07/another-round-of-soviet-era-
humor-ii/

Washington Post. Richard Zoglin. July 5 2020. 'Why do none of Trump's
"jokes" feel like jokes?' https://www.washingtonpost.com/opinions/why-do-
none-of-trumps-jokes-feel-like-jokes/2020/07/03/bdcc053a-bca1-11ea-bdaf-
a129f921026f_story.html Accessed September 20 2022.

Wikihow. "How to Be Funny". By Kendall Jenner. 31 August 2022
https://www.wikihow.com/Be-Funny#Developing-a-Sense-of-Humor
Accessed September 28 2022.

Williams, M., & Emich, K. J. (2014). "The experience of failed humor:
Implications for interpersonal affect regulation." *Journal of Business and
Psychology*, 29(4), 651-668. https:// doi.org/10.1007/s10869-014-9370-9

Willinger, U., Hergovich, A., Schmoeger, M. et al (2017). "Cognitive and
emotional demands of black humor processing: the role of intelligence,
aggressiveness and mood". *Cognitive Processing* 18, 159–167 (2017).
https://doi.org/10.1007/s10339-016-0789-y

Wilson, David and Gervais, Matthew. *Quarterly Review of Biology*, 2005 "The
evolution and functions of laughter and humor: a synthetic approach"
Dec;80(4):395–430. Doi: 10.1086/498281

Winkler, Sasha and Bryant, Gregory. 19 Apr 2021. Play vocalizations and human laughter: a comparative review. *Bioaccoustics,* pages 499–526. https://doi.org/10.1080/09524622.2021.1905065

Wired.com. By Anne Kreamer, March 27 2012. "Creativity Lessons From Charles Dickens and Steve Jobs". https://www.wired.com/2012/03/opinion-creativitydickensjobs/ Accessed September 28 2022.

Yonge C. D. (1853). *The Banquet of the Learned.* London: Henry Bohn. https://archive.org/details/deipnosophistsor03atheuoft/page/n7/mode/2up Accessed September 20 2022.

YouTube.com 22 November 2012. "Reagan Joke—Soviet Union and Getting A New Automobile". https://www.youtube.com/watch?v=CLW7r4o2_Ow Accessed September 20 2022.

Zizek, Slavoj. December 17 2015 "Zizek's Jokes in The Fragile Absolute". zizek.uk:
https://zizek.uk/zizeks-jokes-in-the-fragile-absolute/ Accessed September 10 2022.

Where Did the Jokes Come from?

(Some sources)

Linguist Robert Hetzron offers the definition:
A joke is a short humorous piece of oral literature in which the funniness culminates in the final sentence, called the punchline…In fact, the main condition is that the tension should reach its highest level at the very end. No continuation relieving the tension should be added. As for its being "oral," it is true that jokes may appear printed, but when further transferred, there is no obligation to reproduce the text verbatim, as in the case of poetry. (Hetzron 1991, pp.65–66)

The following are similar instances of the jokes in the book, which, in the authentic sense of jokes and joke-telling, are "up-to-a-point" unique—my own versions often inspired by not one but several jokes, not necessarily these ones.

JOKE #1: Baldy

As the main text indicates, a version of this joke is in the Philogelos, or Laughter Lover, (Hierocles 1983, 11)

JOKE #2: The Joke Book

Again, a version of this joke is in the Philogelos, or Laughter Lover, (Hierocles 1983, 14) but there are more recent, rather different versions of the joke including this one online (Lancaster University, n.d.).

Lancaster University, n.d. "Chuckle Stoop". Accessed September 10 2022. https://www.lancaster.ac.uk/fass/projects/stylistics/topic3a/fun4.htm

JOKE #3: Sherlock Holmes Goes Camping…

"Sherlock Holmes and Dr. Watson Go Camping"

A version of this joke is online. (Sunny Skyz 2013)

Sunny Skyz.2013. "Sherlock Holmes and Dr. Watson Go Camping" February 27 2013. https://www.sunnyskyz.com/funny-jokes/20/Sherlock-Holmes-and-Dr-Watson-Go-Camping Accessed September 10 2022.

JOKE #4: What is an Elephant?

Zizek has a version of this joke on a webpage called "Zizek's Jokes in The Fragile Absolute" (Zizek 2015).

https://zizek.uk/zizeks-jokes-in-the-fragile-absolute/

Zizek, Slavoj. December 17 2015 "Zizek's Jokes in The Fragile Absolute". https://zizek.uk/zizeks-jokes-in-the-fragile-absolute/ Accessed September 10 2022.

JOKE #5: A The Policeman and the Drunk…

A version is online. (Three Quarks Daily 2016)

Three Quarks Daily. March 21 2016 'The "Streetlight Effect": A Metaphor For Knowledge And Ignorance'. By Yohan John.
https://3quarksdaily.com/3quarksdaily/2016/03/the-streetlight-effect-a-metaphor-for-knowledge-and-ignorance.html Accessed September 10 2022.

JOKE #6: Perceptual Spectacles

For example, the version and discussion by E. Bruce Goldstein in the Encyclopedia of Perception. (Goldstein 2010, 492.)

Goldstein E. Bruce (2010). Encyclopedia of Perception. Atlanta: Sage Publications.

JOKE #7: Breaking news
There's a version of this online called "A guy was going on vacation and didn't have anyone to take care of his beloved cat". (Upjoke.com n.d.)
upjoke.com n.d. "Beloved jokes". https://upjoke.com/beloved-jokes Accessed September 10 2022.

JOKE #8: The Elephant
There's a version of this online called "Elephants and Marshmallows". (jokesoftheday.net n.d.)
http://www.jokesoftheday.net/joke-Elephants-and-Marshmallows/201302241

JOKE #9: The Channel Tunnel
See Tommy Cooper's version in his "All In One Joke Book: Book Joke, Joke Book" (Cooper 2014)
Cooper, Tommy "All In One Joke Book: Book Joke, Joke Book" 2014. Cedar Rapids: Arrow.

JOKE #10: The Night Train
There's a version of this online called, "Travel at 60 Daily Joke: A man and woman share a sleeper cabin" (Starts At 60, 2018)
Starts At 60. "Travel at 60 Daily Joke: A man and woman share a sleeper cabin". Jul 04, 2018.
https://startsat60.com/media/travel/train-joke-two-strangers-share-sleeper-cabin-blanket

JOKE #11: A Little Old Lady Goes into the Bank…
See, for example the version online called "Old lady in bank" (Jokes Blogger, n.d.)
Jokes Blogger. "Joke of the Day: Old lady in bank". No date.
https://www.jokesblogger.com/2014/05/16/joke-of-the-day-old-lady-in-bank/

JOKE #12: The Man on the Train to Odessa

See, for example the version online at (americanisraelite.com)

https://www.americanisraelite.com/arts_and_entertainment/joke_of_the_wee k/article_de3346ee-6584-11eb-bb68-5b5367ca4dcd.html (American Israelite 2021)

American Israelite. February 4 2021. "Joke of the Week".

https://www.americanisraelite.com/arts_and_entertainment/joke_of_the_wee k/article_dc3346ee-6584-11eb-bb68-5b5367ca4dcd.html

JOKE #13: The Man Who Thought He Was a Grain of Corn. See, for example, the short version at upjoke.com under the heading "Corn jokes". (Upjoke.com, no date.)

Upjoke.com, no date. Corn Jokes: Guy goes to a therapist. He says, 'Doc, I live in constant fear that I'm a grain of corn and there's a giant chicken out there who wants to eat me.'

https://upjoke.com/corn-jokes#:~:text=He%20says%2C%20%22Doc%2C%20I%20live%20in%20co nstant%20fear,corn%20that%20a%20giant%20chicken%20wants%20to%20 eat.

(The nearest thing to a "title" for the joke is the first line: Guy goes to a therapist. He says, "Doc, I live in constant fear that I'm a grain of corn and there's a giant chicken out there who wants to eat me.")

JOKE #14: Happiness or a Ham Sandwich?

Monroe, Mary 2012 "Deliver Me from Evil", Chapter 24. New York: Kensington Books.

Joke #15: Sartre Orders a Coffee…

See for example (free-funny-jokes.com)

free-funny-jokes.com. "Sartre's Coffee Joke". No date, no author.

https://free-funny-jokes.com/sartres-coffee/ Accessed September 20 2022.

JOKE #16: The Classroom

See for example:

Bestjokehub, no date, no author. Teacher: "Anyone who thinks they're stupid, stand up!" https://bestjokehub.com/joke-94779/ Accessed September 20 2022.

JOKE #17: A woman goes into a railway buffet...
This joke is something of an "urban legend", attributed variously (I think wrongly) to Douglas Adams and a church minister from West Virginia. There are many variations of it on the internet.
Brunvand, Jan Harold 2011. "Too Good to Be True: The Colossal Book of Urban Legends". New York: W. W. Norton

JOKE #18: Attitudinal problems
https://jokes4all.net no author, no date. Pig Jokes.
"Top 10 Jokes about Pigs" https://jokes4all.net/pig-jokes Accessed September 20 2022.

JOKE #19: The New Bicycle
The joke is credited to Ermo Phillips.
BrainyQuote, no date. "Emo Philips Quotes".
https://www.brainyquote.com/quotes/emo_philips_128947
Accessed September 20 2022.

JOKE #20: The New Car
There's a video of this one, Reagan giving it in his inimitable way.
YouTube.com 22 November 2012. "Reagan Joke—Soviet Union and Getting A New Automobile". https://www.youtube.com/watch?v=CLW7r4o2_Ow
Accessed September 20 2022.

JOKE #21: Big Numbers
Feld.com No author. September 22 2005. "Joke Of The Day: How Many Is A Brazillion?" https://feld.com/archives/2005/09/joke-of-the-day-how-many-is-a-brazillion/ Accessed September 20 2022.

JOKE #22: Family Fortunes
As recounted in Ben Lewis' book, 'Hammer And Tickle: A History Of Communism Told Through Communist Jokes,' for example, (Lewis 2011 25)
Lewis, Ben 2011. 'Hammer And Tickle: A History Of Communism Told Through Communist Jokes'. Cambridge: Pegasus 2010
JOKE #23: You Get Just One Wish

See, for example, the version told by Dan Hill of Reuters via The Japan Times. (JapanTimes.co.jp June 11 2015)

JapanTimes.co.jp by Dan Hill. June 11 2015. "Russian president's secrets are right on his face".

https://www.japantimes.co.jp/opinion/2015/06/11/commentary/world-commentary/russian-presidents-secrets-are-right-on-his-face/Accessed September 20 2022.

JOKE #24: The Prisoners
Lewis, Ben 2011. "Hammer And Tickle: A History Of Communism Told Through Communist Jokes". Cambridge: Pegasus 2010

JOKE #25: The Naughty Parrot
bestjokehub.com. No author, no date. Joke-9901: 'A frightened man goes to the secret police and says, "My talking parrot disappeared"'
https://bestjokehub.com/joke-9901/ Accessed September 20 2022

JOKE #26: The Interruption
See, for example (vahshatedil.wordpress.com)
vahshatedil.wordpress.com By Vahshatedil. February 7, 2010. "Another round of Soviet-era humor II"
https://vahshatedil.wordpress.com/2010/02/07/another-round-of-soviet-era-humor-ii/

JOKE #27: Cruelty to Rabbits
See, for example (news.ycombinator.com). By bifrost. February 6, 2017. "CIA Declassified Coldwar Russian Jokes".
https://news.ycombinator.com/item?id=13585511

JOKE #28: Capitalist hell
The joke is in the Prospect Magazine article: "Hammer & tickle". (Prospect May 20 2006)
Prospect. Ben Lewis. May 20 2006. "Hammer & tickle".
https://www.prospectmagazine.co.uk/magazine/communist-jokes
Accessed September 23 2022

JOKE #29: The Longest Queue

For example, see:

Upjoke.com no author, no date. "Gorbachev jokes".
https://upjoke.com/gorbachev-jokes Accessed September 20 2022.

JOKE #30: Stalin's Mustachio
See, for example:
jokes-just-for-fun.blogspot.com No author, no date. "Stalin And Zhukov
Meeting." https://jokes-just-for-fun.blogspot.com/2017/08/stalin-and-zhukov-
meeting.html Accessed September 20 2022.

JOKE #31: Shmoedipus
Koestler, Arthur 1964. "The Act of Creation". Page 33 "The Logic of
Laughter"

JOKE #32: The Spurned Blonde
Time.com October 22 2010 "Sample Some British Humor! The Official List
Of The Best British Jokes" By Frances Perraudin.
https://newsfeed.time.com/2010/10/22/sample-some-british-humor-the-
official-list-of-the-best-british-jokes/

JOKE #33: Life of Brian
No author, no date. "Life of Brian Script: Scene 3: Jesus' Lack of Crowd
Control on the Mount"
http://www.montypython.50webs.com/scripts/Life_of_Brian/3.htm

JOKE #34: The Survival Kit
No author, no date. 'The 100 Scariest Horror Movie Moments of All Time: Dr.
Strangelove or: How I Learned to Stop Worrying and Love the Bomb (1964)
Slim Pickens: Maj. "King" Kong'
https://www.imdb.com/title/tt0057012/characters/nm0001620

Sources for the Puzzles

PUZZLE NUMBER #1: is Stick or Switch?
See (ucsd.edu), "Let's Make a Deal: Monty Knows". No author, no date.
https://mathweb.ucsd.edu/~crypto/Monty/monty.html?_ga=2.73327251.1828
253864.1663673562-1848398046.1663673562

PUZZLE NUMBER # 2: The Parking Space

See (mentalfloss.com)

A version online is at (mentalfloss.com)

"What Is the Car's Parking Spot Number?". Alvin Ward.

February 28, 2018.

https://www.mentalfloss.com/article/533625/parking-spot-brain-teaser

PUZZLE NUMBER #3: The Riddle of the Sphinx

See (mythologyexplained.com)

A version online is at (mythologyexplained.com)

mythologyexplained.com. "The Sphinx Riddle: The Story of Oedipus and the Sphinx in Greek Mythology" No author. No date.

https://mythologyexplained.com/oedipus-and-the-sphinx-riddle/

PUZZLE NUMBER #4: Who calls?

A version online is at (futilitycloset.com)

futilitycloset.com. November 19 2005. "An International Riddle".

https://www.futilitycloset.com/2005/11/19/an-international-riddle/

PUZZLE #5: The Elusive Mistake

This is a variation on the ancient theme of the paradoxical nature of self-referential statements. I discuss this in my own book 101 Philosophy Problems (Third edition). (Cohen 2007 118)

Cohen, Martin. 2007. "101 Philosophy Problems: 3rd edition". London: Routledge.

PUZZLE #6: The Puzzle of Logical Time

This is based on the version offered by Jacques Lacan in his essay 1945s "Logical Time and the Assertion of Anticipated Certainty". (Baily et al 2018, pages 141)

Bailly, Lioner et al. 2018. "The Lacan Tradition". Abingdon: Routledge.

PUZZLE #7: The Man Who Got Stressed Out By A Piece of Paper

See, for example, the version called "Piece of Paper on the Cactus" at PuzzleWocky.com.

(PuzzleWocky.com)

PuzzleWocky.com No author, no date. "Situation Puzzles".

https://puzzlewocky.com/brain-teasers/situation-puzzles/

PUZZLE #8: The Ambiguous Death of Ronald Opus

Apparently, the case was originally told by Don Harper Mills, then president of the American Academy of Forensic Sciences, in a speech at a banquet in 1987. The story was reported by Snopes.com a decade later. (Snopes.com)

Snopes.com 20 December 1999. "1994s Most Bizarre Suicide". https://www.snopes.com/fact-check/1994s-most-bizarre-suicide/Accessed September 24 2022.